Walks in Herefordshire, Gloucestershire and Worcestershire
Three Choirs Counties

Roy Woodcock

Published by Sigma Leisure – an imprint of
Sigma Press, Stobart House, Pontyclerc, Penybanc Road
Ammanford, Carmarthenshire SA18 3HP

British Library Cataloguing in Publication Data

A CIP record for this book is available from the British Library

ISBN: 978-1-85058-901-3

Typesetting and Design by: Sigma Press, Ammanford, Carms

Maps: © Bute Cartographics
Contains Ordnance Survey data © Crown copyright and database right 2012

Photographs: © Gordon Whiting

Cover photograph: Worcester Cathedral from the road bridge © Gordon Whiting

Printed by: Berforts Group Ltd

Disclaimer: The information in this book is given in good faith and is believed to be correct at the time of publication. Care should always be taken when walking in hill country. Where appropriate, attention has been drawn to matters of safety. The author and publisher cannot take responsibility for any accidents or injury incurred whilst following these walks. Only you can judge your own fitness, competence and experience. Do not rely solely on sketch maps for navigation: we strongly recommend the use of appropriate Ordnance Survey (or equivalent) maps.

Contents

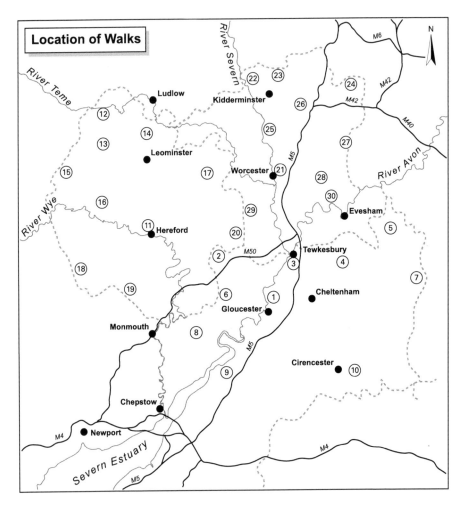

	Area (sq. kms)	Population
Gloucestershire	2,653	582,500
Herefordshire	2,180	178,000
Worcestershire	1,741	555,500

Highest points

Gloucestershire	Cleeve Hill	330m
Herefordshire	Black Mountain	703m
Worcestershire	Worcs. Beacon	425m

Introduction

The Three Counties contain some of England's finest scenery consisting of undulating lowlands, with upstanding hills including the well known Cotswolds and Malvern Hills, the Lickeys, Forest of Dean and several prominent hills of Herefordshire. Much of the landscape has been strongly influenced by geology, notably rock type and earth movements. The oldest rocks are the pre-Cambrian rocks of the Malvern Hills and the very old Cambrian rocks of the Lickeys, whilst the hills of Herefordshire towards the Welsh Borders are younger, mainly Silurian and Devonian in age. Gloucestershire contains old Devonian and Carboniferous rocks in the Forest of Dean area, but in the east are the Cotswolds where the distinctive limestone rocks are of Jurassic age.

The lower areas are the river valleys, mostly draining towards the south. Worcestershire is crossed by the Severn (220 miles in length) and its main tributaries the Avon (96 miles) and Teme, and the main Herefordshire river is the Wye (130 miles in length and the 5th longest in the UK). Like the Severn, it rises on Plynlimon in mid Wales but they diverge to follow different routes before meeting again in the Severn estuary near Chepstow.

Much of the three counties drains to the south and the Severn Estuary, but the eastern part of Gloucestershire on the gentle dip slope of the Cotswolds drains to the east – with the Thames and many of its tributaries such as Evenlode, Windrush, and Churn adding to the scenic beauty of the area.

The rivers were enlarged by melt water at the end of the Ice Age and this contributed to the formation of the valleys, but the Ice Age also contributed to the landscape by dumping surface deposits, especially on the lowlands. Small glaciers and freeze-thaw activity contributed to changes on hillsides where small steep valleys were created, as can be seen in the Malverns and elsewhere.

But on top of the physical landscape are features of vegetation and settlements, which create their own type of landscape. Wild lands and forests were removed for farming although several large woodland areas survive in the Forest of Dean and Wyre Forest, and many small woodland areas are found on hillsides and areas of poor soils not very suitable for farming.

The three counties are mainly rural, with urban areas in the three county towns as well as Cheltenham. Parts of north Worcestershire around Kidderminster and Stourbridge have industrial pasts, as has the Forest of Dean. In spite of the rural and scenic similarities there are marked differences too.

Gloucestershire the largest, consists of three distinctive areas, the Cotswolds in the east, the Severn Valley in the middle and the Forest of Dean in the west, alongside the Welsh Borders. Each of these three can boast attractive scenery ranging from the stone villages of the Cotswolds to the flat lands alongside the Severn and extensive woodlands of the Forest of Dean.

Worcestershire is mainly rural and contains beautiful countryside. The hills around the edges, Malverns, Abberley, Lickeys and Cotswolds create a saucer-like shape, with lower land in the middle. The hills are of old hard rock, except for the Cotswolds which are much younger. Dotted around the county are hill forts, battlefield sites, canals and nature reserves, some of which will be passed on the walks included in this selection.

The largely unspoilt and even more rural county of Herefordshire is a land of hills and vales creating glorious countryside. The main hills, the Malverns and Black Hills, are located on the eastern and western margins. The main river is the Wye, with the Lugg, Frome and Arrow as tributaries. Black and white villages as well as old forts and castles are numerous, and the fields of orchards and cattle give a characteristic landscape of the county.

Acknowledgements

My thanks to Gordon for accompanying me on all of these walks and taking such a good selection of relevant photographs. Also thanks to Margaret for coming on many of the walks and reading through the proofs of the walks, checking on accuracy and improving the wording in many cases.

1. Gloucester

This is partly an urban walk enjoying a little of Gloucester's history. Start from the old dock area, now all modernised with the large warehouses preserved and put to various uses such as flats, offices and museum. Our circuit takes us out of town and along the river bank on Alney Island, part of which is a nature reserve and occasionally covered by flood water.

Distance and time	4 miles; requiring 2 hours plus any time spent on visiting museums, the cathedral or other features of Gloucester's history
Terrain	Gentle and mostly flat with firm paths, but possible problem with floods at certain times of the year, normally in winter
How to get there	Follow signs into Gloucester City Centre and then the sign to the Historic Docks, where there is a large car park
Starting point	At the docks, grid ref 828182
Refreshments	Choice in the docks and a wide choice in the City centre
Tourist Information Centre	In Gloucester (phone 01452 396572)
Nearby places of interest	Forest of Dean; Painswick and Slad in the Cotswolds
Maps	OS Landranger 162; Explorer 179

Gloucester grew as a crossing point of the Severn, helped by the fact that the river splits into two branches which were easier to bridge, and downstream the river becomes tidal. The settlement existed in pre-Roman times but growth came as they developed Glevum to

Main dock basin

control the river crossing. Growth continued throughout the centuries and many rulers came here, and most Tudor Kings held parliaments here. The street plan and remnants of walls date from Roman times and the Cathedral dates from 1089. Most of the city is situated to the east of the river, and crossing points and floods have been an ongoing problem.

As Britain's most inland port, Gloucester relied on the Severn. Port status was granted by Queen Elizabeth I. Meanders, shifting sand banks and the Severn bore hindered navigation, and to improve navigation downstream the Gloucester-Sharpness canal was opened in 1827. In the Docks, 1846 was a big year when three warehouses were built to handle grain imports following the Repeal of the Corn Laws. Altogether a total of 15 warehouses were built giving some indication of the importance of river and canal traffic. The Main Basin is now surrounded by old warehouses which have been modernised and put to use as shops, bars, cafés and new modern flats.

The walk

1. Start from the North End of the docks, close to the large lock which enables boats to get from the River Severn into the Main Basin of

the Dock and along the Gloucester-Sharpness canal. Walk past the North Warehouse (built in 1826 by the Gloucester-Berkeley canal company) and the old manually operated crane on the left, and then on the right is the former warehouse now used by the council. On the wall is a plaque, first of many to be seen in Gloucester. Turn right and walk over the bridge which can open up to allow boats to enter the Victoria Dock to the left. Pass the small Mariners chapel, dwarfed by the large size of the warehouses. The first service here was held on 11th

Mariners Chapel

February 1849 and there are still regular Sunday services. Walk across the large open area and pass the small Albion Cottages on the left, now the centre for Visitor Information and Docks Management and Security. Walk southwards towards the new shopping area with smart outlet shops. But before then, pass the National Waterways Museum in Llanthony Warehouse on the right with café, gift shop, starting point for boat trips, etc. then the small Coots Café and onto the road and turn right.

This leads to the Llanthony bascule bridge from where there are good views back to the Docks or along the canal to the south. At the end of this road, with Inn on the Docks on the right and the large Gloucestershire College on the left, turn left along the modern south-western bypass. Walk a short distance alongside this busy road to reach the site and ruins of Llanthony Secunda Priory. This was built here at a time that the original Augustinian Llanthony Priory in Llanthony valley in South Wales was seized by rebels in 1136. Amongst many important visitors was Edward II who stayed here on his way to Berkeley Castle. The Priory was dissolved in 1538 and little now remains. The information board shows how it might have looked in mid 15th century. The ruins and grassy areas occupy the space between the main road and the canal, and the site is looked after by the Llanthony Secunda Priory Trust.

2. Retrace steps along the main road, and cross to the left side of the main road, Castle Meads Way. Pass over the river and soon reach a footpath where you turn sharp left signed to Over, Highnam Scenic Route and Cycle Track 45. This leads down and away from the road along a surfaced path which soon bends right. To the left

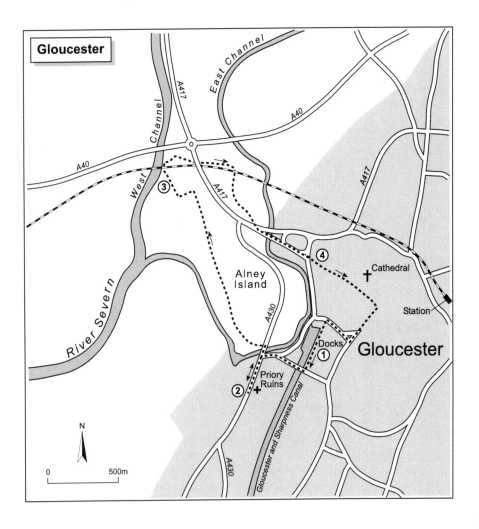

is the old footbridge across the river. And also to the left, off the path is an old canal lock and a house dated 1879. Reach a cattle grid and a metal kissing gate and the sign for the Alney Island Nature Reserve. Pass a windmill beyond which are wonderful views to the Cathedral tower and St Nicholas church. The river is away to your left and the Electricity Transforming Station and rugby pitch to the right. This open area of rough ground is an ideal location for plants and animals. The surfaced path has become a stony path but still firm and dry (except in flood times of course). Pass beneath the power lines to reach another cattle grid and kissing gate. At a junction of tracks, go slightly left, still following Cycle Route 45. Cross the remnants of an old railway line and pass to the right of a large warehouse. Go on past another cattle grid and the path turns right. See a small pond to the left and then go through a small gate before passing beneath the bridge carrying the railway line across the river. A few more yards along the path and before reaching the main road, noisy with traffic, turn right along a grassy path. But first, go left up onto the old disused road bridge. This is a Telford Bridge which dates from 1825-28 and replaced an old 13th century bridge – but has now been replaced by modern road bridges. An information board at the far side of the bridge gives a little historical information about Telford. His bridge spans the Maisemore channel of the Severn, and was the lowest bridge across the Severn until the high bridge at Aust was built in 1966.

3. Leave the bridge for the onward route, pointing to Gloucestershire Way and Wysis Way. Enjoy the good views to the Cathedral. The path at first is grassy and through undergrowth, but soon goes alongside the railway to reach a footbridge signed Gloucestershire Way and Three Choirs Way. Stay on the right side of the field until reaching a point where you can pass beneath the railway line. Walk through a Millennium decorated iron gate and, when the path soon divides, take the left fork and pass through the open woodland, which has a variety of deciduous trees. This leads through to a small metal gate, by a larger gate, and straight ahead to reach the main road close to the 'Welcome to the City of Gloucester' sign. Walk along the left side of this road for 30 yard then fork left to follow the footpath sign to the City Centre. Soon go right, beneath the eastbound lanes of the main road, to reach the narrow cycle

way and a bridge over the Severn. This path divides, left to the Boating Lake, but you go right. Cross the west bound lanes of the main road, and continue towards the City Centre. When the road bends right towards the Docks, keep straight ahead towards the Cathedral. Cross the main road with care to reach Westgate Street and keep straight ahead.

Pass the Folk Museum, which is housed in 16th and 17th century Tudor and Jacobean buildings. Here can be seen displays of Pin Making, Gloucester and the Civil War, old fishing methods and local agriculture including how to make Gloucester cheese. Across the road on the left is St Nicholas, which dates from the 12th century. The spire was originally taller but was hit by artillery fire in the Siege of Gloucester in 1643 – and became unsafe so was shortened to half of its former height. Keep ahead, to the wide and spacious pedestrianised area, with open air cafés. The imposing Shire Hall designed by architect Robert Smirke, in 1816, is to the right, but even more imposing is the Cathedral down College Street to our left. A few yards down College Street is the medieval gate and entrance to the cathedral precincts and a small building known as King Edwards Gate, where the body of King Edward was received by the Abbott – after his murder at Berkeley Castle in 1327. Another route to the cathedral from Westgate Street is along the narrow alley called College Court leading past the Beatrix Potter Tailor of Gloucester Shop. St Michael's Gate is close to this shop – it was the entrance gate used by pilgrims visiting the shrine of Edward II.

4. After visiting the Cathedral continue along Westgate into the centre of the town at the Cross. Here is a tall church tower, the only surviving remnant of St Michael's

Cathedral

church. Turn right along Southgate Street, and notice the second shop on the left, Bakers Watchmaker and Jeweller, with the wonderful chiming clock. Pass the statue of Emperor Nerva on a horse, and then the Tourist Information Centre, as you leave the pedestrianised road and join the traffic again. On the left is St Mary de Crypt, parts of which date from Norman times. George Whitefield (1714-1770), who with Charles and John Wesley helped to establish Methodism, was baptised and confirmed in this church. He was a great preacher who preached his first sermon here in June 1736, but subsequently crossed the Atlantic thirteen times in order to preach in the USA. Robert Raikes (1736-1811) also had links with this church. He founded Sunday Schools, as a means of educating children who worked in factories all day long on weekdays – and he lived in the recently restored house opposite the church.

Join a busier road (still one way only) coming in from the right and, in a few more yards, leads to a road junction with traffic in both directions. Turn right and cross over here and walk along the left side of the road towards the River Severn, passing warehouses on the left, including one used as the Soldiers of Gloucestershire Museum. Good views of the dock area can be seen between the buildings as you walk along this road and, on reaching the large lock linking the Dock Basin with the Severn, turn left here to enter the docks from this point.

Chiming clock in Southgate Street

2. Kempley

The walk crosses glorious countryside to be enjoyed at any time of the year, but is at its best when the wild daffodils are in flower. The route is across fields and along lanes rich in wild daffodils in spring, with visits to the two churches of Kempley.

Distance and time	5 miles; time required 2½ hours
Terrain	Gently undulating and may be wet underfoot in winter. Several small stiles on the route
How to get there	From Ledbury take the B4216 to Dymock, turn right past the Beauchamp Arms and the church then first left (signed to Kempley). After a few yards cross over the route of the old railway line and turn right. About two miles along this narrow road reach a T-junction and turn left (signed to Newent) and a mile along this road is the starting point in Queen's Wood
Starting point	GR677285 – at a parking area in Queen's Wood
Refreshments	Pubs in Dymock and Much Marcle
Tourist Information Centres	Ledbury (01531 636147) and Ross on Wye (01989 562768)
Nearby places of interest	Large tree in churchyard Church at Much Marcle; the Westons cider museum; Dymock church and the exhibition on the Dymock Poets
Maps	OS Explorer 189; Outdoor Leisure 14; Landranger 149

Noted for its wild daffodils, the area is also famous for the group of poets who lived in or visited this area. Fields used to be full of daffodils and visitors came by train loads to gather armfuls of the flowers. After the fields were ploughed up to grow crops, daffodils were restricted to field margins and lanes although a few grassy fields still have large clumps of the wild flowers each spring. The Daffodil Way is a signed path linking Kempley with Dymock and the route follows part of this Daffodil way. Also near Dymock are two signed Poets Paths which pass the houses where the Dymock Poets lived in the years 1911-1916 and across the countryside over which they walked seeking inspiration (and sources of cider). The group of six poets Lascelles Abercrombie, Wilfred Wilson Gibson, John Drinkwater, Rupert Brooke, Robert Frost and Edward Thomas lived in or visited the area in the years before World War I. Much of their writing was about the countryside and several poems referred to the daffodils.

John Drinkwater wrote:

> *Because brave daffodils you bring*
> *Colour and savour of a spring*

The walk

1. Queen's Wood is managed by the Forestry Commission and on the notice board is a map and signs for forest trails. Start from the parking area, by walking out on to the road and turn left and walk towards Kempley. Pass the village sign and keep ahead along the road. Shortly beyond the point where the Daffodil Way is signed to the right, pass a few houses on the left, and look for the Daffodil Way sign to the left. Turn here to go through a modern metal gate and straight ahead close to the right margin of the field. This leads downhill slightly, to reach a double stile. Daffodils line many of the field margins in this area. Go on over a stiled footbridge and through another field. After another stiled footbridge, turn left, with the house and garden on the left, to reach a stile where you turn right for a few yards. Go through a wooden gate to pass to the left of the stables. Once beyond a gated stile and footbridge, head straight across the field to reach a stile. Continue ahead, along the left margin of several fields and over the stiles, until reaching the road.

2. Turn right, and at the road junction fork left. Walk along the road for about 500 yards and just beyond the bridge and the small river, turn right over the stile, still following the sign for the Daffodil Way. The path winds along the field margin, with Kempley Brook on the right. Reach a stile and just keep ahead following the stream and keep close to the field boundary. Ignore a footbridge going to the right and soon reach a footbridge on your path. Keep straight ahead, staying by the hedge and the stream. At the end of the next field, where there is a footbridge to the right, do not turn right but keep ahead through a gap in the hedge and straight across the next field to reach a stile and the road at a road junction. On the small

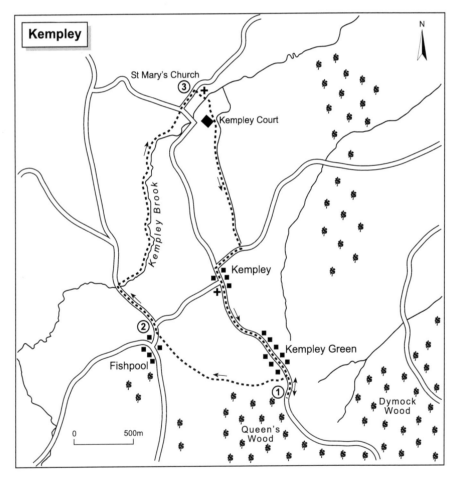

island in the middle of the road stands a memorial tree planted on the 20th February 1893 by the Vicar and Parishioners of Kempley in commemoration of the coming of age of the William 7th Earl Beauchamp of Madresfield Court Worcester-shire. Continue straight ahead, along the road signed to Dymock, to reach Kempley old church.

3. This could be considered as an alternative parking and starting point. Walk through the churchyard of St Mary's Kempley, but pause here to have a good look round this exquisite 11th or 12th century Norman church. Wall paintings are from the 12th century – some of the oldest in Britain. The tower is dated 1276 and was built for defence, with no entrance from the outside. The amazing variety of features of interest inside include roof timbers dated from 1150 by dendrochronologists – the oldest timbers in any church in the United Kingdom. Daffodils are abundant in the churchyard. Walk on the left side of the church and leave the churchyard through the gate and go ahead across the

St Mary's 11th century church

Carvings on the wall of St Edward's

stiled footbridge over Kempley Brook. Pass to the left of the large barn and on over another stiled footbridge. Follow the hedge on the right margin of the field, as far as a stiled footbridge where you turn right and then immediately left. Go on through a large metal gate and along the left side of the field to reach a track. When this track bends left keep straight ahead with the hedge on your left, to walk along the margin of a very long field. Reach a stile and the narrow road where you turn right. At the T-junction turn left and soon reach the Kempley newer church. St Edward The Confessor dates from 1903 having been built as a Chapel of Ease, and as a replacement for the old church which was considered too isolated and liable to flooding. Only consecrated in 1934, this is another delightful church. Built of local stone from the Forest of Dean and using local timber for roofing and the large beams, the church was funded by Earl Beauchamp and designed by Randall Wells, the brother of H.G. Wells. There are impressive carvings on the exterior wall, and a Rookery in the churchyard. Walk on along the road, passing the Village Hall (where tea and home made cakes are served on Daffodil Sunday) and a clear map of the Poets' Paths and Daffodil Way on a map in the layby. Pass by the houses of the village, going on beyond the turning on the right where you walked earlier, and shortly reach Queen's Wood and the starting point.

3. Tewkesbury to Deerhurst

The walk takes us along the tree lined River Severn as well as visiting the historic village of Deerhurst and learning a little of Tewkesbury's eventful history, on this gentle circuit.

Distance and time	6 miles, with an extra mile round part of the town. Time required 3-4 hours
Terrain	Mostly flat with only one gentle climb, but there may be muddy patches along the riverside and in the fields
How to get there	Tewkesbury is on the A38 between Worcester and Gloucester, and close to junction 9 on the M5
Starting point	Car park alongside Gloucester Road just south of the Abbey on the main road out of town. Grid ref. 888323
Refreshments	Very good choice in Tewkesbury
Tourist Information Centre	Tewkesbury (phone 01684 855040)
Nearby places of interest	Malvern and the Malvern Hills; Upton-on-Severn
Maps	OS Landranger 150; Explorer 190

Tewkesbury is an ancient settlement, named after a Northumbrian monk Theoc or Theuk who created a cell here. The Abbey was founded in 1092 and consecrated in 1121. Although now only a parish church, the Abbey Church of St Mary, it is larger than several of the English cathedrals. The abbey was closed by Henry VIII in 1541, but at the dissolution of the monasteries the local people bought the abbey to save it from destruction. An earlier important date in the local history was 4th May 1471, the Battle of Tewkesbury, when the Yorkists gained a victory in the Wars of the Roses.

Deerhurst is rare in having a Saxon Minster, now the parish church, and also the ancient Saxon chapel. Odda's Chapel dates from 1056, and had become part of the adjacent large farmhouse, until being rediscovered in the 19th century. It was then cleaned up, having been used as a byre, and has been restored to show the pre-Norman architecture. St Mary's church dates from the 7th century and large and small stones were placed in alternate layers, in typical Saxon style. There was a monastery here from 804AD, and parts of the building survive from that time, although there was major restoration work in the 10th century. The Priory House next door to the church is mainly 14th century, and is located on the site of the original Priory which extended across the lawn in front of the house. The small settlement of Deerhurst has always suffered from flooding and an old embankment near the river has helped to reduce flood danger. A larger embankment was built during 2009-2010.

The Walk

1. From the car park on the road out of town, walk over Swilgate and cross the end of Lower Lode Lane – straight ahead along the main road to pass the Council Offices on the right. Turn right along Lincoln Green Lane, signposted to the Golf Course. After a few yards turn right through a wooden kissing gate (signed Battle Trail) into the Bloody Meadow – a rather worn looking information board tells us much about the history of this area, and the bloody Battle of Tewkesbury. Walk through the lush flower rich meadow to emerge onto the narrow lane – Lower Lode Lane – and turn left. With the large ham (the word meaning an area liable to flood) on your right you soon reach the point where the Mill Avon joins the Severn, by a parking and picnic place, with Lower Lode Inn on the opposite bank. Walk downstream and pass the boathouse of Cheltenham College. There are flood level heights on the doors – 1947 and 2007. Pass through a gate and head southwards, walking close to the river in a narrow field at first and then larger fields. These fields are liable to flooding in the winter, and over to the left on the top of a short steep slope is the woodland named Long Plantation – which you shall walk alongside later. Pass through a gate and the church in Deerhurst comes into sight. Continue downstream until reaching a stile and a former crossing point of the river.

2. Before reaching a small boatyard, and Yew Tree Inn, on the
   opposite bank, turn left to cross the field towards the buildings of
   Deerhurst. Notice the embankment in this field, built up many
   years ago to reduce the risk of flooding in the village. Go through
   the gate into a small car park, and there is Odda's Chapel – which
   is now looked after by English Heritage. The notice board explains
   that this small Anglo Saxon chapel, which shows several
   characteristic features of late Anglo Saxon construction, was built
   by Odda, a kinsman of King Edward the Confessor, in memory of
   his brother Aelfric. Walk along the road and pass the very smart
   Odda's Barn next door, where B and B is on offer. The road bends
   round to the right and passes the flood barrier which can be closed

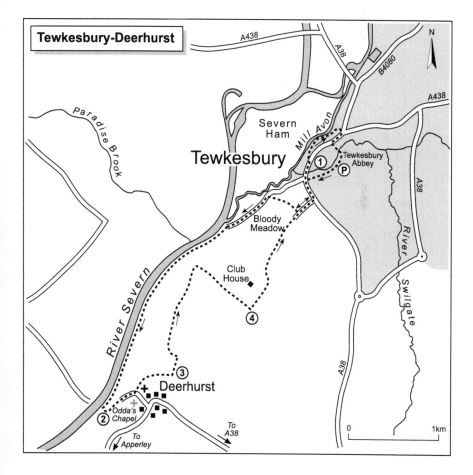

whenever necessary. Then turn left to walk through the churchyard, passing another, though smaller, new flood barrier, and noticing Priory House on your right. The church is very special with many features of interest, including the famous angel, a Saxon sculpture on the outside of the east end, where the remains of the apse can also be seen. Inside can be seen an ornate Saxon font, a memorial to a dog and also memorials to the Strickland family from Apperley Court, as well as many architectural features. After looking for the angel round the back continue through the churchyard, beneath the large redwoods and the noisy rookery. Other birds are abundant in this area and the churchyard is covered with snowdrops in early spring, then bluebells and ladies smock. A large scheme (2009-2010) to protect Deerhurst from flooding has made slight changes to the landscape as you leave the churchyard – and slight changes to the footpath. Leave the church-yard through a new gate and walk alongside the large barn to another small gate. Cross a farm track and go on through another metal gate, to walk along the embankment which grad-ually bends round to the right. Walk on over a narrow ditch and keep straight ahead across another field –

Odda's Chapel

Priory church of St Mary

and still on the embankment. Reach a footbridge with small 'V' stiles at each end.

3. Once over this turn left, along the field margin with the hedge on your left. At the end of the field go over a stiled footbridge and turn left for a few yards but follow the field boundary as it bends round to the right. Pass a pond on your left, and then go over a stile – and turn left. Follow the field boundary and begin to bend to the right, to reach a wooden stile. Go straight on here, and begin to climb steadily. Follow the edge of the field with the woods on the slope to the left, which you saw earlier from the river bank. The path climbs at first but then levels off. Keep straight ahead for just over a half mile, with occasional views through the trees down to the river and the plain beyond. When the path eventually bends round to the right, reach a footpath sign after a few yards, and a stile into the golf course. Do not turn left here but just follow the field margin with hedge and golf course to the left. Follow the margin of the golf course and, when you reach a hedge at the end of the field, move a few yards right to a gate, and then left a few yards, but really just keeping straight ahead. At the end of the next field, turn left over a stile and footbridge to enter the golf course.

4. Pass, but take note of the warning notice about danger from golf balls, and head straight across the course, following the yellow topped marker posts. Pass the shelter for the driving range and enjoy the landscape of the golf course but also the glorious views to the Cotswolds. Pass the 11th Tee and then head diagonally left, following the direction of the arrow. Climb slightly as you cross a fairway to reach the narrow road, where you turn right. Across to the left can be seen Tewkesbury Park house, which dates from the 18th century, having been built on the site of the 14th century house belonging to Edward Despenser, whose family memorials can be seen in the Abbey Church. Follow this driveway slightly downhill to walk away from the Club House and back towards Tewkesbury. Pass the entrance to the Bloody Meadow where you walked earlier and turn left at the main road to return to the starting point.

If time is available, a short walk round part of Tewkesbury is recommended to round off this walk. This suggestion is shown as an extra small circuit on the map.

4. Hailes Abbey

Surrounded by glorious scenery, climb up the Hailes Valley to walk along the Cotswold ridge top before returning across grazing land back into the valley.

Distance and time	5 miles, with a short cut option of only 3 miles if required. Time: 2½ hours or less than 2 hours if using the short cut
Terrain	Clear and firm track then narrow road to climb steadily up onto the Cotswolds, before descending steadily through fields of pasture, back to the Abbey
How to get there	Along the B4077 Tewkesbury to Stow-on-the-Wold road, turning off southwards at Toddington crossroads, signed to Winchcombe. After one mile along this road, the B4632, turn left following the sign to Hailes
Starting point	Near Hailes Abbey: Grid ref. 051301. Park close to the abbey and the church (if visiting), or park at Hayles Fruit Farm (with permission – phone 01242 602123)
Refreshments	Hayles Fruit Farm (open 9-5) or nearby in Winchcombe
Tourist Information Centre	Winchcombe (01242 602925)
Nearby places of interest	Winchcombe and Sudeley Castle
Maps	OS Explorer OL 45; or Landranger mainly on map number 150 but just extending onto 163

The Cistercian Abbey at Hailes was founded in 1246 by Richard of Cornwall, brother of King Henry III - and dissolved in 1539. A major attraction for pilgrims was the Holy Blood of Hailes, allegedly a phial of Christ's blood. Owned by the National Trust but managed by English Heritage, it is open daily from April to October, and provides a very clear and informative audio tour, with extra information in the museum. The small church opposite is built of local stone, and has an unknown dedication. It predates the abbey, having been built about 1130. The old font dates from the 13th century, as do the wonderful wall paintings. Outside in the churchyard is the Hailes Labyrinth, historically used by anyone to walk round quietly and think or meditate. A labyrinth differs from a maze in having only one path which winds round and into the centre. The same route is used to leave the labyrinth.

The walk

1. Walk past the Abbey along the narrow road, which soon begins to climb. As it bends to the right, on its way to Hayles Fruit Farm, Farm Shop and Restaurant, keep straight ahead here, following the sign for Cotswold Way, a public bridleway which follows the line of an ancient track, lined with stones. The steady climb is in a shady area, with woods on the left, and an abundance of springtime flowers in the verge as well as in the woods. Bird song is likely to be noisy in spring and early summer. The wood continues on the left, as fields and orchards can be seen to the right. This valley is an ideal location for orchards, being sheltered and south facing. The danger of frost in blossom time is reduced by the sloping ground which enables cold and frosty air to roll downhill to the plain.

2. As you come into more open land above the woods, reach a cross paths, where the Cotswold Way goes left to Beckbury Camp and Stumps Cross, and the onward route leads straight ahead to Farmcote.

   For the short cut option turn right over a stile and follow the public footpath sign. Head a few yards to the left, then bend right to walk alongside a hedge and begin to descend. There are lovely views all round, both close by in the Cotswolds but also to more distant hills including the Malverns. Look for a sign where you move right, to the other side of the hedge, but continue in the same direction with the hedge now on your left. Reach a farm track and move to the right for a few yards and then go left, following the arrow – with the hedge and small stream on your right. This leads down to another track where you turn left in a few yards and then right to descend to a small ford. Beyond here turn to the right and then head left diagonally and climbing slightly, across an orchard to reach a finger post and a footbridge at the far side. Keep ahead into another orchard, heading diagonally across to the far corner of the orchard close to an old barn. Leave the field in this corner, along a grassy

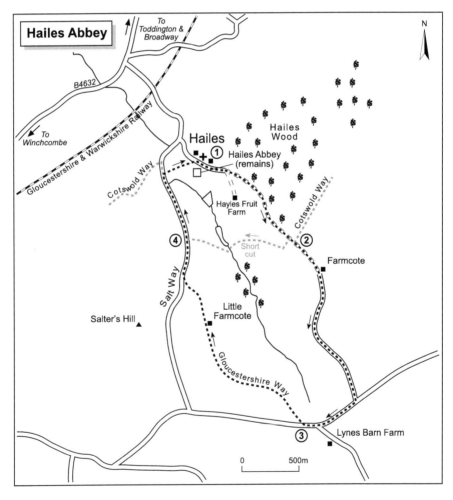

Hailes Abbey ruins

track, but after a few yards go left, over a stile and across a narrow field to another stile and the narrow road at point 4.

The main route keeps straight ahead at point 2, still climbing steadily to reach Farmcote. Pass between the fine stone buildings – with a chance to buy herbs and chilli peppers if required. The small stone roofed church of St Faiths is to the right. Only the nave survives from the old Norman church, as the chancel was demolished. Now out in the open and along a level road, you can enjoy good all round views, but may feel exposed in harsh weather. Reach a road junction and fork right towards Winchcombe – and descend slightly. At the next road junction two paths go right and you ignore the first of these. But take the second path signed Gloucestershire Way, going through a large gate.

3. Once in the field, bend left following the track which leads round to the right side of a large barn. On the right down the slope can be seen evidence of some strip lynchets, evidence of ancient farming. Reach a stile by a gate and keep straight ahead close to

the margin of the field - with woods to the left. Go over a metal gate and into an area of trees, to reach a gate and enter a large field. A wooded slope is to the left, and fields of pasture extend down to the right. Across the valley you can see the route of the earlier part of this walk. Stay close to the left side of the field and walk on towards the farm buildings ahead - this is Little Farmcote. Go through a gate and aim to pass to the right of the large barn. In the left corner of this smaller field go over a stile and into a farmyard. Turn right to pass between fine stone buildings and some large barns, and out onto the surfaced farm road - gated here, to control the movement of animals. This leads steadily downhill to join the road, Salter's Lane, which follows the route of an ancient Salt Way. Proceed down here, enjoying the views across to Hayles Fruit Farm in the valley.

Ancient wall paintings in Hailes church

4. Pass a stile where a path comes in from the right, and this is the route of the short cut option. Follow this road beyond a cattle grid and soon reach a few lovely stone houses on the right. Turn right at the end of these, along Cotswold Way to a gate and then cross the grassy field, with the ruins of Hailes Abbey to the right. The lone stone cross in the field is possibly the location of the gateway where Pilgrims would have entered the original abbey. Go through the kissing gate and on to the road, directly opposite the old church.

5. Chipping Campden

Walk round part of the town and then out into the surrounding countryside with a stroll to Dover's Hill to enjoy the glorious views across the Vale of Evesham to Cheltenham, Malvern and the Clee and Clent Hills.

Distance and time	4 miles; requiring 2-3 hours
Terrain	Gentle in the town and only a slight incline up to Dover's Hill – it is the dip slope of the Cotswolds and not the steep escarpment
How to get there	Turn off the A44 3 miles east of Broadway, along the B4081 to the car park at the Sports Centre and School, close to the church
Starting point	Near the church (GR155395). An alternative parking and starting place is on Back Ends at point 2 of the walk (GR148392)
Refreshments	A very good choice of pubs, cafés and hotels in the town centre
Tourist Information Centre	On the High Street opposite the Market Hall (phone 01386 841206)
Nearby places of interest	Broadway and Snowshill
Maps	OS OL 45; Landranger 151

One of the most famous and most attractive of the Cotswold towns and villages, a small settlement had grown up at Chipping Campden before the Norman Conquest. Chipping, meaning market, and Campden probably derived from valley with camps or enclosures. A market charter was granted by King Henry II in 1185 and this contributed to the town's growth. Sheep farming brought prosperity in the 14th and 15th centuries and William Grevel was one of Britain's most successful merchants – and a major financier for building the fine wool church of St James. A major benefactor in the 17th century was the local lord Sir Baptist Hicks who lived in Campden House – which was burnt down in the Civil War – and never rebuilt.

With the decline of agriculture the town declined. But fortunately, with a railway line, and several empty cottages, the town was given a boost by the arrival of members of the Arts and Crafts movement. CR Ashbee considered Chipping Campden ideal for his plans, and he relocated the Guild of Handcrafts here in 1902. He moved from the East End of London with many skilled craftsmen, and set up a workshop in the Silk Mill in Sheep Street. Although most of the craftsmen had moved back to London by 1908, their short stay in the Cotswolds encouraged the growth of the Arts and Crafts movement in this area, making imaginative use of old crafts and producing hand made articles, drawing upon rural areas for ideas and inspiration. The Guild went into liquidation in 1908 but by then the tradition had been established and still continues today. Ashbee left in 1919 and Griggs became the principal figure between the two World Wars.

Lodge gates

Dover's Hill was bought by Frederick Landseer Griggs, an etcher and engraver who came to live in Chipping Campden in 1904. He realised the hill was threatened with development for a large hotel. He later passed the hill to the National Trust who have been managing the area since 1929. The hill is named after Robert Dover (1582-1652), a local barrister, who organised the Olimpick Games here in 1612 and they continued, with a few gaps (such as the Civil War) until 1852. They were stopped then for a variety of reasons including rowdy behaviour and some of the games were becoming too violent. They were revived in 1951 and are still held annually – nowadays on the Friday evening after the Spring Bank Holiday. Competitions include sack races, tug of war, and shin kicking.

The magnificent parish church of St James mostly dates from the 15th century, but a few earlier fragments have survived. A major donor was William Grevel (who may have been the inspiration for Chaucer's Merchant pilgrim). There is a memorial brass to Grevel, and many other monuments, including the 17th century tomb of the Hicks family in the South Chapel. The approach to the church is along the avenue of lime trees, representing the Apostles. Also in the churchyard can be seen several graves of the Arts and Crafts workers.

The walk

1. Start from the church and walk towards the High Street. On the left are the ogee shaped gate lodges, surviving remnants of Campden House. The house, built in 1613, was burnt down by Royalists. Also on your left is Court Barn Museum, a museum of Craft and Design. Here can be seen the history of silver, jewellery, bookbinding, printing, cabinet making and other crafts (open daily except Mondays). On your right we can see the Tithe House and next the old Alms Houses, built by Hicks in 1612. Approaching the main street look ahead at the roof line and the variety of buildings. This is a very photogenic main street. The town motto is History in Stone – which is most appropriate, as most of the buildings are built from local stone, many dating from 16th 17th and 18th centuries. Walking along the left side of the main street you pass Woolstaplers Hall, built in the 14th century by Robert Calf, a medieval wool merchant. The Ashbees came to live here in 1902, and in here Woodroffe, noted for his work in stained glass designed a window

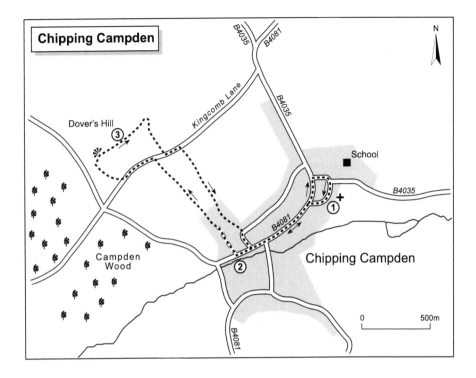

with ash and bee! Moving on, pass Lygon Arms, Dovers House where Griggs lived from 1906-1930, and the Old Grammar School. The Noel Hotel has a carriageway route through the building , and on your right by now is the island in the middle of the road, with the Old Market Hall. This was built in 1627 by Sir Baptist Hicks to provide shelter for stallholders selling their local produce. An early example of a farmers' market. It had been owned by the Noel family, and was bought for the National Trust in 1944 and subsequently re-roofed. Also on the island between two roads, is the War Memorial, designed by Griggs, and a small parking area. Beyond this is the Town Hall, 14th century in origin but largely rebuilt in the 19th century – dated 1897. Pass the Red Lion, before Sheep Street and on the next corner is the Robert Welch show room, situated in the Old Silk Mill. This is the location of the starting point of the Arts and Craft Revolution in Chipping Campden when CR Ashbee and his Guild of Craftsmen moved to the town in 1902.

Continuing along the main street, where every house is of interest and holds more of the history, you reach Izod House which looks old but was built by CR Ashbee for an old Campden farming family.

2. Cross over here and turn right, walking away from the main street, with St Catharine's Roman Catholic church on the right and delightful immaculate gardens on the left. When the road divides, with Back Ends going right (there is car parking here – and it may be used as an alternative starting point for the walk), and Hoo Lane, the route of your return from Dover's Hill continues straight ahead. But fork left along Birdcage Walk to begin the gentle uphill walk to Dover's Hill (225m – 738 ft). After a few yards of tarmac turn right along a narrow path between hedge and fence. Reach a road and move 20 yards to the left, and then turn right on a footpath. Cross a footbridge over a small stream to reach another road, and keep straight ahead. Go on through a kissing gate into

Inside the Market Hall

an old orchard - probably with grazing sheep - stay close to the fence and reach another gate, then cross the middle of a field – another former orchard. Walk along the edge of a small field to a gate and into a large field and go straight across to reach a road, Kingcomb Lane. Turn left here and walk along the verge for 250 yards to a footpath sign and go right, through an old gate. Cross the field and then go over a stile on to the open grassy area at the summit of Dover's Hill. A very useful Information Board can be seen in the car park, and the toposcope points out a few of the features to be seen in the glorious viewpoint. A natural ampitheatre is down below us and the panoramic view opens out across the plain.

3. Walk on from the toposcope, with the steep Cotswold scarp to our left, and a line of trees and the field crossed earlier to your right. Stay close to the line of trees and walk towards the triangulation point. A few yards beyond this on the right is a gate, where you turn, along a narrow path, now following the Cotswold Way. Reach the road and turn left for about 100 yards and then turn right. A clear track leads down to farm barns and then the first rather impressive houses on the edge of Chipping Campden. Pass more of the lovely stone houses and on the right notice three with thatch, the last of which contains a large topiary bird in the garden. You are now at the end of Hoo Lane and its junction with Back Ends. Keep straight ahead to reach St Catharine church (point 2 again) and turn left along the main street.

Walk along the left side of the road passing yet more lovely stone houses. A few yards beyond St Catharine School is the Davies House where a plaque tells us that was the birthplace of Ernest Wilson in 1876. He became known as one of the world's largest plant collectors, from all parts of the world but most notably from China. Elm House is on the left, and was formerly an important building as the school for the Arts and Craft movement. When the road divides, stay on the left side – with the island on your right. Here are restaurants, the Town Hall, War Memorial and the Market Hall. Of many more old buildings on your left, be sure not to miss the Old School House, with the cane logo on the door post, and the weird Punk sculpture on the doorstep. Dating from 1977 this remarkable figure was shaped from Forest of Dean sandstone. Just beyond Miles House, formerly two 17th century cottages, on the opposite side of the road is the Ernest Wilson Memorial Garden – with a collection of trees and shrubs gathered from all parts of the world – and a fitting tribute for a great botanist. Then turn right towards Ebrington on Cidermill Lane, the B4035, to complete your tour and return to the car park and the church.

Market Hall from the outside

6. May Hill

Climb steadily up through glorious woodlands and emerge to a stunning view over the Severn Estuary before continuing the climb across the grassy area which surrounds the tree capped summit. All round views take in the Malvern Hills, Sugar Loaf near Abergavenny, hills of Wales and into Shropshire, before the gentle descent back down to the starting point.

Distance and time	4.5 miles – 2-3 hours
Terrain	Steady climb most of the way up to the summit, mainly on paths through the woods, some of which may be muddy in wet weather; the gentle descent is on grassy paths through scattered trees and ending up along the narrow road
How to get there	Turn into Newent from the crossroads where the B4215 meets the B4221 and take the first turn to the right signed to the Bird of Prey centre. Once beyond the Bird of Prey Centre follow signs to the tiny hamlet of Cliffords Mesne. Fork left towards Glasshouse and then look for the right turn signed to the Yew Tree Inn
Starting point	Yew Tree Inn (permission required to park): GR 699227
Refreshments	Yew Tree Inn (phone 01531 820719) – closed on Mondays
Tourist Information Centre	Ledbury (01531 636147)
Nearby places of interest	Museum in Newent; Birds of Prey Centre; Ross-on-Wye; Three Choirs Vineyard
Maps	OS OL 14; and Landranger 162

The walk

1. Just in Gloucestershire, the walks start is only a few yards outside Herefordshire. Turn left from The Yew Tree Inn, and walk down to the T-junction, at May Villa, then turn right along the road. Look for the footpath sign on the right, at the edge of the woods. Turn right here, into the Huntley Estate on a track leading through a grove of redwood trees. The track soon divides and you follow the right fork. A yellow arrow points straight ahead, and at a second yellow arrow the path begins to climb. Cross a horizontal track and

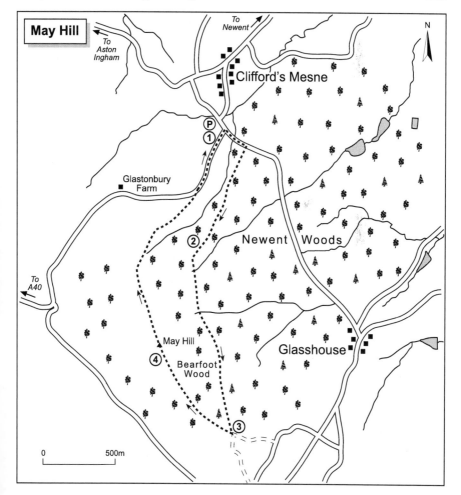

keep climbing – in deciduous woodland now. The track has a stony base, but may be muddy and leaf covered. The path levels off and at a T-junction reaches an area of young trees. Turn right along a major track. After about 50 yards the track divides and you keep straight ahead – heading south and climbing. Follow a broad track on the edge of the more recently felled patch then bend right along a fairly level stretch.

2.
When this track divides, with a gate and footpath sign to the right, go left and start climbing again – heading south and enjoying wonderful views left to Malverns, Bredon Hill, Clee Hill and other landmarks. Reach a broad major track and turn left, into an area prolific in sweet chestnuts in the autumn. The path leads on with slight undulations but is generally fairly level. You may notice a 'Walkers are Welcome' sign on the left. Pass three left turns and a sharp right turn but just keep ahead, passing an area of coppicing. At a large beech tree in an open space, where five paths meet – is the time of decision. The first path on the right to a marker post and another 'Walkers are Welcome' notice leads through the trees up to the grassy area which surrounds the clump of trees on the

View to the Severn estuary

top of May Hill. But the recommended path is ahead and to the right, as it leads through the woods to a gravel path and the sudden opening up of views over the meandering Severn as it widens out towards its estuary.

3. At the gravel path turn right and climb gently up to a metal gate and signs for Wysis Way and Gloucestershire Way. There is a National Trust sign too, as the summit area is in the management of the National Trust, with 4 acres (1.6 hectares) at the summit a Site of Special Scientific Interest (SSSI) managed by Longhope Parish. Walk up the grassy area, through scattered gorse bushes, as the grass widens out. Horses are often used to help control the vegetation here and all around the summit. Enjoy further views to the Severn Estuary, Edge Hill with three masts located just north of Cinderford, Sugar Loaf over beyond Abergavenny and other hills to north. Just before the clump of trees is the stone built triangulation point, and inside the trees is a plaque mentioning some of the history of the trees – planted by Longhope Parish Council and replenished in Queen ELizabeth II Jubilee Year in 1977 by the May Hill Preservation Society.

4. Although only 296m (970 ft) in height, this prominent landmark with its summit group of trees is a well known feature, being clearly visible from the M5 as well as from miles of surrounding countryside. The summit trees include Corsican pines planted in 1888 to celebrate Queen Victoria's golden jubilee (1887). More trees were added to celebrate Queen Elizabeth's silver jubilee and still more for the Queen Mother's 80th birthday. This cap of trees is meant to be long lasting, as replacements for the future are already growing. This well known landmark has been featured by many writers in the past.

Ivor Gurney wrote:

> *May Hill that Gloucester dwellers*
> *'Gainst every sunset see.*

And John Masefield in his *Everlasting Mercy* wrote:

> *Above the plains of Gloucester,*
> *She lifts her rounded head.*

Move on in a northerly direction following the main grassy path beginning to lead downhill – with trees over to the left and to the right. Veer slightly towards the edge of the trees on the right to reach two gates – one leading to the woods which you ignore. Go on through the other gate slightly to the left of the wood and here join the recently created Geopark Way. From this gate is a choice of paths through scattered trees and grass and bracken. It does not matter which path is followed as they all lead to the narrow road, but probably best is the middle path and then veer slightly to the right following an open grassy path. Reach the road and turn right, cross over the cattle grid and walk along the road to return to the Yew Tree Inn.

Scattered trees on the descent

7. Adlestrop

From the beautiful stone village walk across glorious countryside, passing close to Chastleton National Trust House as well as crossing through Adlestrop Park.

Distance and time	5.5 miles. Time required about 3 hours
Terrain	Undulating with a gentle climb up to Adlestrop Hill. Along country lanes and clear paths, which may be muddy in places especially the wooded areas
How to get there	Along the A 436 from Stow-on-the-Wold towards Chipping Norton, then turn left into the village about 4 miles east of Stow
Starting point	GR242272 at Adlestrop Village Hall
Refreshments	Village Post Office or back to the pubs in Upper or Lower Oddington (the Fox Inn at Lower Oddington phone 01451 870555) – and a very good choice in Stow
Tourist Information Centre	Stow-on-the-Wold (phone 01451 831082)
Nearby places of interest	Stow; Daylesford church with its memorial to Warren Hastings, a former Viceroy of India
Maps	OS Explorer OL 45; Landranger 163

The small stone village of Adlestrop is worthy of note in its own right, but was made more famous by the poem written by Edward Thomas, one of the Dymock poets, a group who gathered in Dymock for friendship and inspiration in the years before World War I. His train from Oxford to Worcester on 23rd June 1914 made an unscheduled stop close to Adlestrop station.

Yes. I remember Adlestrop
The name, because one afternoon
Of heat the express train drew up there.
Unwontedly. It was late June

Many of the houses in the village are built of attractive mellow yellow Cotswold stone.the church of St Mary Magdalene has an unusual tower, with a clock which only has faces on two sides – those which face the village. A church has existed on this site for centuries but most of the present bare and simple building is from the 18th century. The chancel arch is the oldest part dating from the 13th century and the tower is 14th or 15th century. Monuments to the Leigh family can be seen in the church and the churchyard, as they were the owners of the Adlestrop Park Manor House from 1553 onwards. Opposite the church is the 17th century Adlestrop House; formerly the Rectory, and occupied by the Rev. Thomas Leigh (1726-1813) a cousin of Jane Austen's mother. Jane visited the house on at least three occasions, and scenes written in Mansfield Park are based on her visits here.

Chastleton is a nearby village seen on our walk. The church of St Mary is on the site of a pre-conquest church but the present church still has Norman remnants in the12th century doorway and arched pillars. Other features of interest include medieval floor tiles in the South Aisle chapel, wall paintings on the north wall and floor brasses close to the lectern. One of these is a memorial to Katharine Throckmorton, grandmother of Robert Catesby. Adjacent to the church is the Jacobean Manor House, built by the wealthy wool merchant Walter Jones. He bought the house and estate in 1604 from Robert Catesby, who led the gunpowder plot. Jones demolished the house and built a replacement between 1607-1612. Some work and repairs were made in the 18th and 19th centuries, but the house deteriorated during the 20th century because of a lack of money. The family sold the house to the National Heritage Memorial Fund in 1991, and the

The old railway sign in the bus shelter

National Trust took over the care and management of the house. Extensive restorative work took place before the house was opened to the public in 1997. Much of the work is for conservation rather than restoration, as the Trust aims to retain the house and contents as they were in the past. Visitor numbers are limited by the use of timed tickets for admittance. Outstanding amongst a large number of interesting features are a secret room, and the long gallery, together with the garden and the croquet lawn.

The walk

1. Leave the village hall parking place and turn left, and after a few yards turn left again along the stony track. Follow the signs for the Macmillan Way and Diamond Way heading northwards towards Chastleton. The Macmillan Way is a cross country route passing through the Cotswolds, and the Diamond Way is a 60 mile circuit in the northern Cotswolds. The track leads to a stile by a gate beyond which the path divides. Take the left fork across a flower meadow to a stile by a gate in the corner of the field. Keep straight ahead by the fence on the left, but after 30 yards go over the stile and continue ahead. Reach a stile by a gate and cross a long field, slightly uphill leading towards a wood. Go over the stile and through a small wood, then across the middle of a field to a metal gate.

   The edge of the National Trust Chastleton Estate is beyond the gate and there is a choice of three paths. Turn right along the edge of Peasewell Wood and notice over to the left the good views to the Dovecote (dating from 1751) on four legs and beyond is Chastleton House. Keep straight ahead, over a low stile then through a wooden gate and begin to climb slightly through woodland. The path levels off and at a gate turn right. A few yards to the left at this point is a narrow road, which leads down to Chastleton House – and well worth a visit if you have time. It is easily accessible by car, but prior booking may be necessary (phone 01608 674981).

2. Having turned right, go over a stile (where there may be a notice advertising tea, coffee and cake in Adlestrop Post Office). Ignore the left turn but keep straight ahead, as views open up to the west,

towards Evenlode, Broadwell and Stow. Head south along Adlestrop Hill, in an area where skylarks are likely to be seen and heard in spring and summer. This hill is also noted for other birds as well as butterflies. Pass a lone seat and viewpoint and continue along the level path. Reach a small wood on the left and keep straight ahead along the margin of the field. Soon turn right, still following the edge of the field. In the next corner of the field move a few yards to the right to reach a small gate. Go on through here along a path between lines of trees, and this path becomes a track which leads us through to the road. Turn right along the road and descend slightly to walk down to the village. Pass a horse warning

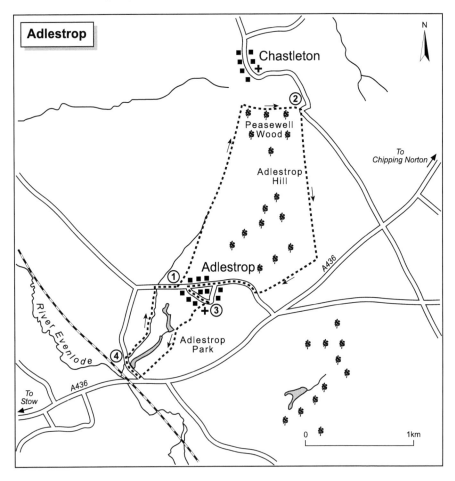

sign, as horses are numerous in the adjacent fields – with the stables of Richard Phillips being situated at Adlestrop. Reach the road junction where, in the bus shelter, is the old railway station sign from the former station mentioned in the Thomas poem. It was possibly not one of his best poems but he was one of the most famous of the First World War poets – and he was killed in 1917.

We are only about 50 yard from our starting point at the Village Hall, but turn left, to walk through the village. Pass stone houses, with colourful gardens and then reach the Post Office with its thatched roof. The road divides here.

3.   Keep ahead along the right fork, passing a large gate to the Manor House, and the church of St Mary Magdalene on the left. The Coachman's Cottage is on the right, and the former rectory which is now Adlestrop House – the house visited by Jane Austen. Pass between the church and Adlestrop House to walk along the

Stone houses in the village

bridleway between stone walls. Reach a gate and a small kissing gate, and then another gate with a pond to the right, as you emerge into Adlestrop Park with the cricket pitch straight ahead. This glorious parkland was created by Humphry Repton, and looking back and to the left can be seen a big manor house, the home of the Leigh family.

The driveway runs along the left side of the cricket pitch. As it begins to bend left over towards the Lodge House, go right off the surfaced drive just beyond a short line of massive oak trees extending to the right, and head across the parkland, following a slight hollow along a sunken path way. Reach a wooden kissing gate and, after a few yards of rough ground, another gate, to reach the road. A few yards to the left is the main A436, with the railway line and the location of the famous station close by. But turn right along the narrow road.

4. Pass the gate to the Adlestrop lake used by Moreton Angling Club and just beyond here reach a smart wooden kissing gate. Turn right and follow the right margin of the field, with views across to Adlestrop Park over to the right. Leave the field by going right, over a newish wooden footbridge, and through a wooden gate. Cross the field and keep ahead to reach the road. Turn right, pass the driveway to Lower House Farm and Adlestrop stables, to arrive back at the Village Hall on the left.

8. Forest of Dean

This circuit from the Speech House walks through rich mixed forests, along part of the Gloucestershire Way and Beechenhurst Trail, passing through an arboretum and alongside the Cannop Ponds.

Distance and time	6.5 miles - 3 hours
Terrain	Can be muddy in places but with good firm paths in places too
How to get there	3 miles west of Cinderford along the B4226
Starting point	About 100 yards along the road B4226 from the Speech House in the Arboretum car park. GR. 623123
Refreshments	Speech House (phone 01594 822607); Beechenhurst Lodge Visitor Centre (phone 01594 827357)
Tourist Information Centre	Coleford 01594 812388; Dean Heritage Centre at Soudley 01594 824024
Nearby places of interest	Sculpture Trail; Symonds Yat
Maps	OS Outdoor Leisure 14; Landranger 162

The Forest of Dean is still sometimes known as the Queen of Forests and oaks cover a quarter of the large forested area. Other common trees include Douglas fir, spruce, larch and pine. As a royal hunting forest it was used by Norman Kings and as early as the 11th century Verderers were appointed to look after the animals and the forests.

The Verderers Court still meets, and hold their meetings in the Speech House. The court was always known as the Court of Speech - hence the name of the hotel. The Speech House was built in 1676 by Charles

II for use as a Hunting lodge. His arms can still be seen above the exit door to the Verderers Court, and the Lodge is now a hotel.

The Beechenhurst Visitor Centre is open daily in summer and at weekends in winter, and was built on the site of the former Speech House colliery, where coal was mined from 1847-1906. The mine covered over 2000 acres underground and employed 500 men and boys in the 1880s. The mine closed in 1937, and then a picnic site was created in 1969. Later, work began to create a Visitor Centre opened in 1992 by HRH the Duchess of Kent. The smart Visitor Centre makes good use of local stone and there are solar panels on the roof. An extension and the new Gavellers Café was opened in 2008. The first Gavellers were appointed in about 1244 with the responsibility of receiving revenue from the miners in the Forest of Dean. Since 1924 the Forestry Commission has been the Gaveller.

The walk

1. From the Forestry Commission car park alongside the arboretum, walk through the gate into the Cyril Hart arboretum, named after the local historian and forestry expert. A very good information board stands just inside the entrance. The collection was begun in 1910 and now has more than 200 species – mostly named and with level walking suitable for disabled and elderly visitors. The Passage of Time sundial is near the entrance – and there are other wooden carvings. Created originally in 1915 as an experiment to see what would grow, the arboretum was founded by Ernest H Wilson, a famous plant collector, although the name was changed in 1999 to the Cyril Hart Arboretum. Dr Hart was a Senior Verderer who had a long connection with the Arboretum.

    Once through the entrance turn right to walk through the arboretum – notice the large cricket field and the Speech House out of the wood on your right. Leave the arboretum though a tall gate, pass a parking area to the left and reach the narrow road. Turn right here to walk along the verge to the Speech House. On the left are the Royal Oaks planted in 1957 by Queen Elizabeth II and the Duke of Edinburgh, and said to have used acorns taken from a tree planted by Elizabeth I. Close by is a memorial stone to Albert the Prince Consort, dated 1861. Cross the B4226 opposite

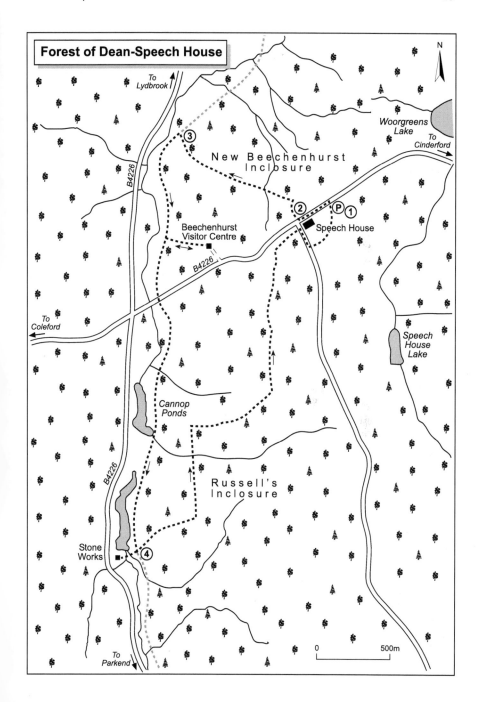

the Speech House to the stone pillar located in what was regarded as the centre of the forest. Renamed after Lord Bledisloe in 1957 on his 90th birthday, it commemorates his 50 years as a Verderer.

2. Follow the sign pointing to the Gloucestershire Way and walk away from the road, slightly downhill along a grassy path through bracken. After about 100 yards go left through a small gate and immediately right into the trees. On the left are yew trees close to a memorial stone commemorating the coronation of Edward VII in 1902. Go on downhill slightly to a cross tracks with a stile to the right – but we turn left following the yellow arrow and walking in a westerly direction. Pass a marker post with a blue ring and look for the memorial tiles which floor a short section of the track. Reach a junction of five ways and keep straight ahead (short cut to Beechenhurst is on the signpost) along a broad and stony track. On your left pass a huge wooden chair on a prominent point with good views over the surrounding forest. The chair is called 'Place',

Looking along Cannop Ponds

by Magdelena Jetelova (1986), and is part of the Sculpture Trail. Begin to go downhill passing a post with a blue ring to reach a major cross tracks. A left turn here leads to Beechenhurst Lodge, with refreshments if required, but the onward route for the walk is straight ahead, towards Speculation and the Heart of Stone, following the red route. After about 100 yards reach another cross tracks and keep straight ahead, and downhill. Soon a left turn for the blue route leads a few yards to a stone sculpture, the Heart of Stone, by Tim Lees (1988) on the site of a disused drift mine. After detouring to the sculpture return to the route continuing downhill and then up slightly to a gate and a track – a cycle route along the embankment of a former railway line. Turn left, and enjoy the easy walking along a level and firm track.

3. Pass a sign pointing right to the Cycle Centre but keep straight ahead signed to 'Cannop Wharf 2.6kms'. Along this next stretch it is possible to diverge to the left up to the Visitor Centre if required, but the onward route takes you southward following the cycle track. Reach a road, the B4226, and keep straight ahead. This leads through to a narrow road where walkers, cyclists and motorists all share the route. The first of the Cannop Ponds is to your right, and you soon reach a parking and picnic site where there may be a refreshment van. Keep straight ahead along the cycle route and the second of the Cannop Ponds will be on your right. The ponds were created by damming Cannop Brook in 1826, to provide water for the works downstream at Parkend. The ponds are now home for many birds and a popular picnic and walking area. The Cannop Valley was an area where oaks were planted on the orders of Nelson at the time of the Napoleonic Wars – but by the time they reached maturity iron had replaced wood for ship building – so more softwoods were planted.

4. At the southern end of the ponds turn left, at the sign for 'Cannop Wharf 61m'. and a signpost pointing to Parkend straight ahead or left for Dilke Bridge. But first, detour right along a narrow footpath, across the dam at the southern end of Cannop Ponds to look at the Stone Works (phone 01594 562304). Opened in 1902 this is the only active stone works in the Forest of Dean. Across the road (B4234) is Bix Slade, a sandstone quarry in use intermittently since the 13th century. An old tramway was still used until 1947

and remnants can still be seen. After detouring along the path to the right to look at the stone works, return to the signpost pointing to Parkend and Dilke Bridge. Start on the path towards Dilke, but after less than 10 yards turn left onto a path through a small wooden gate, signed for Gloucestershire Way and the Beechenhurst Trail, with red ring, yellow arrow and green dot. The narrow path through bracken and trees soon reaches a cross tracks where you turn left at the red ring and arrow and signs for Gloucestershire Way and Beechenhurst Trail. The red route soon goes left through a small gate, but keep straight ahead along the broad stony track and climbing slightly.

Just before top of the ascent turn right signed with a yellow arrow, Gloucestershire Way and green dot for Beechenhurst Trail. Climb slightly and keep straight ahead at a cross tracks, to reach a major junction with five routes – the left one is partially overgrown. Turning slightly left, follow the main stony track and the yellow arrow and GW and BT signs. On a level stretch as the track is bending to the right, go left, following the yellow arrow, and still on the GW and BT. The grassy track winds through large trees and then narrows to a path. Traffic noises may be increasing ahead. Reach a stile over a fence and turn right along a narrow path. Just before reaching the road, turn right – still on GW with yellow arrow and green dot, walking through bracken and trees including some fine old oaks. Pass a magnificent beech on the right – the Mahony Beech, with a memorial plaque in appreciation of Brian Mahony's service as Deputy Surveyor. Reach the road at a junction, directly opposite the Speech House, at point 2. Either turn right to retrace steps through the Arboretum, or walk along the road passing the front of the Speech House to return to the starting point.

View of Speech House

9. Berkeley-Sharpness

Cross fields from the historic town of Berkeley to the docks at Sharpness, before returning along the river bank.

Distance and time	7 miles requiring about 3 hours
Terrain	Mostly level, but may be muddy in places
How to get there	From the A38 south of exit 13 on the M5, and along the B4066 signed to Berkeley
Starting point	GR 683994, in a car park in the centre of the town
Refreshments	Good choice in Berkeley including the Berkeley Arms Hotel, a fine 18th century building
Tourist Information Centres	Stroud (01453 760960) and Gloucester (01452 421188)
Nearby places of interest	At the northern end of Sharpness Docks is the starting point of the Sharpness-Gloucester canal. In Berkeley is the castle, the church and the Jenner Museum
Maps	OS Explorer 167; Landranger 162

Berkeley is a small Georgian town which grew around the church and castle. The church of St Mary the Virgin dates from 1100 but the only remains from that time are the Norman door and Norman font. Most of the church was rebuilt in the 13th and 14th centuries. Mural paintings date from the 14th century although they were restored in Victorian times. Many memorials to the Berkeley family can be seen in the church. In the churchyard are the graves of George and Mary Thorpe, grandchildren of the founders of Berkeley Virginia, as well as Thomas Pearce the Watchmaker who was mayor of Berkeley five times. A separate tower in the churchyard stands on the site of a Saxon church.

The Castle dates from 1153, when Lord Maurice Berkeley built his fortress here on the site of an earlier castle (1067). Local stone was used, including some very red sandstone. The Norman keep survives but most of the present building dates from 14th century. The Fitzhardinge family and now the Earls of Berkeley have lived here for 900 years. Berkeley is a famous name not only in London, Berkeley Square, but also in California with Berkeley University. Amongst many attractions in the castle are a collection of fine paintings, the historic Great Hall and the Norman keep with the dungeons and cell where King Edward II was murdered in 1327. The castle also contains a tropical Butterfly House set in the walled gardens. (Castle phone is 01453 810332)

Adjacent to the church and castle is the Edward Jenner Museum (open in summer – phone 01453 810631). Dr Edward Jenner (1749-1823) developed the vaccine for the feared disease of smallpox, which killed up to 20% of the population. He can possibly be regarded as the man who saved more lives than anyone else with any other medical discovery.

The walk

1. From the car park walk back to the crossroads close to the Town Hall and turn right along Salters Street to walk out of the town. Pass a few shops and houses and the Mariners Arms and the Boars Head. After about half a mile, as the road bends left, turn right along Hook Street passing the caravans and chalet houses. Just beyond Porlock House at the end of the lane, bridleways diverge and you take the left fork. This leads to a grassy track (which may be a little overgrown in summer) between hedges before

Berkeley Town Hall

emerging into open countryside. Views open up across to the power station and navigation lights on the river bank. Reach an old iron gate, and walk on through a narrow field. Note a pond on the right, and reach the corner of the field to pass through two iron gates onto a stony track. Pass to the left of Oakhunger Farm and the farm track becomes a narrow surfaced road. Pass a footpath going off to the left and keep ahead along the driveway. On your left is the old Saniger Farm with plaster inscription of 1718, and a stone barn dated 1854.

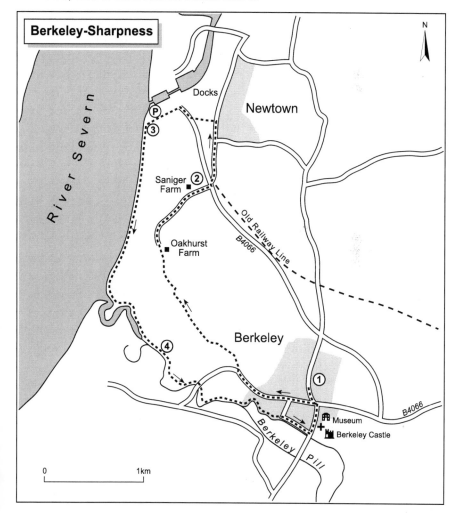

2. Reach the main road B4066 and turn left towards Sharpness Docks. After 30 yards turn right beneath the railway bridge. Walk along the pavement and, when the road bends right, keep straight ahead along Oldminster Road. After 100 yards turn left along the footpath which is part of the Severn Way. A narrow surfaced path takes you across the old railway line and through small gates to reach another road, where you turn right. As this road bends right into the docks, turn left, signed to the Picnic area. Close to the decorated former church on the left, turn right to the picnic area, the viewpoint and the large lock for boats wishing to enter the docks. Telford probably designed the canal entrance lock into Sharpness Port, and the Gloucester-Sharpness canal was opened in 1827. A visitor notice board will give both tidal and shipping information, including some of the cargoes, such as wheat, cement and fertiliser. Enjoy the views across the wide river, to the cliffs and woods and a railway line running along the shore. Lydney is situated across the river here and the tiny entrance to the harbour and a few masts of the yachts can just be seen. Leave the entrance to Sharpness Harbour and walk across the grass,

Sharpness Harbour

past the two rows of houses and the Coastguard Station for the onward walk.

3. Go over a stile by the footpath sign for Severn Way, and head southwards along the river bank. Follow the embankment with the river on the right and the large works to the left. The condition of the tide will determine how much mud is showing, but this coastal strip is likely to contain a good variety of bird life at any time of year or tide, including land birds such a skylark, pipit, kestrel and water birds such as gulls and oystercatchers. Walking southwards provides good views to Berkeley Power Station, with Oldbury station in the distance, as well as the two high bridges crossing the river.

Soon pass the sewage farm on our left, and then a navigation light. Across the river is the entrance to Lydney Harbour. The path begins to bend left along the Berkeley Pill and away from the Severn, as you approach Berkeley Power Station. This was the first commercial nuclear power station in the UK, producing electricity from 1962 until 1989. It was defuelled by 1992 and is now being decommissioned. The site was chosen where ample flat land was available for a large building and close to the Severn which supplied adequate water for cooling requirements, even at low tide.Two white beacons are across the Pill to your right, as you move away from the Severn. Follow the embankment as it bends left, alongside the Berkeley Pill, a tributary river channel, which was used in the past for transporting cargoes up to Berkeley, including stone for Berkeley castle. Reach an iron gate with an interesting catch (test your IQ ??), and bend right – along the embankment. Straight ahead up on the Cotswolds can be seen an obelisk beyond the church and castle in Berkeley.

4. Reach a gate and a sluice, and turn left here, before the gate. Still following Berkeley Pill on your right, continue along the field margin to a stile by a gate in the far right corner. Follow the line of the pill on your right, and then swing left along the field boundary, towards the right side of a large warehouse. Go on over a stile near the end of this building and along a narrow path, with a small river still alongside. Wind along this path to a V-shaped stile, and the road. Head straight across, through the kissing gate

and walk to the right of a house and garden. Go on over a stile and along the right margin of the next field, to a modern metal gate. Cross a small field to another modern metal gate. Across to the right is an old mill and chimney – and ahead is a much clearer view than previously of the Tyndale monument on Nibley Knoll. A stream is to your right and a wire fence to the left. Cross over a small footbridge, and emerge into the open, with houses on the left. Keep straight ahead, past a small pumping station and children's playground. The path becomes gravelled, as the castle becomes clearer in the view ahead. The stream is still to your right as you cross the end of a road and then along a surfaced lane (Jumpers Lane) which takes you through to a T-junction. This is the main road into the town centre and you turn left here. As you walk back to the starting point, the castle, and then the church and the Jenner Museum are a few yards to the right.

The Jenner Museum

10. Cotswold Water Park

The walk follows a canal towpath and former railway line as well as along the Thames path. We pass through South Cerney and close to the smaller Cerney Wick, both of which take their name from the River Churn, a tributary of the Thames.

Distance and time	Nearly 8 miles; time required about 3 hours
Terrain	Flattish and gentle and although most paths are firm and dry there may be muddy patches. Only four (easy) stiles on this walk
How to get there	Along the A 419 between Cirencester and Cricklade - turn at Spine Road Junction B4696 to reach the Cotswold Water Park Gateway Centre (open daily 8-5)
Starting point	Grid ref. 072971
Refreshments	Gateway Centre and the Old Boathouse Gastro pub next door; pubs on the route in South Cerney and Cerney Wick
Tourist Information Centre	Keynes Park Visitor Centre (01285 868096)
Other places of interest	Nearby towns of Cirencester and Cricklade
Maps	OS Explorer 169; Landranger 163

Cotswold Water Park covers 40 square miles in Wiltshire and Gloucestershire and contains over 140 lakes - ten of which have been designated as SSSIs. Geologically this is a large area of gravel brought by melting ice in the Ice Age and resting on top of Cotswold limestone. Water gradually flows through the gravel from north to south and when gravel has been extracted the water fills the holes to create lakes. Sand and gravel have been extracted since the 1920s and as work continues new lakes will be created. With so many lakes it is possible to use them for all kinds of activities and each activity can have its own special space without competing or clashing with others. The lakes are numbered and some have restricted use e.g. for sailing, water skiing, fishing, bird watching. The area is noted for its wild life, especially birds. Thousands of visiting waterfowl are present in the winter, and in summer ducks and waders nest here together with summer visitors such as warblers, swallows, swifts, hobbies. Twenty three species of dragonfly have been recorded and fourteen species of bats. Flowers are abundant and this is a good walk at any time of year, with the lakes, rivers, fields, small woods and wetlands.

The walk

1. From the Gateway Centre cross the car park to reach the canal side, where an information board tells us some history of the Thames-Severn canal built to link Lechlade with Stroud. Turn right along the canal towpath to walk towards Cerney Wick. The canal was opened in 1789 and enabled Stroud, Gloucester and the Midlands to trade with London area. The canal closed in 1933 and restoration work began in 1972. The good and firm path, lined with daffodils in spring, takes us alongside the canal, passing Cotswold Outdoor Action on our right and a lake (number 6). On your left is a large lake (86). Reed beds along the canal and rich vegetation provide homes for birds and insects

18th century Round House

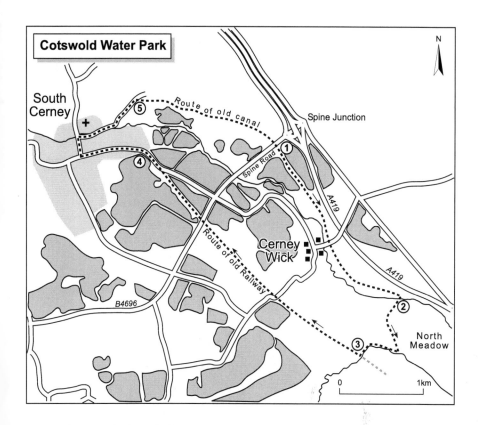

and the whole of the Cotswold Water Park is one large nature reserve. A path goes right, to the River Churn, but keep ahead to Cerney Wick. Adjacent to an old lock pass the interesting Round House, built as the Thames-Severn canal maintenance man's house in the 18th century.

Cross a narrow road, and along this road to the right is the small village of Cerney Wick with its excellent pub, The Crown (phone 01793 750369). Keep ahead alongside the canal, the county boundary at this point – with Wiltshire to the left and Gloucestershire to our right. Pass a newish lake (97) on the left and an old stone wall on the right of the path. Look carefully at these stones and many will reveal fragments of shell as all the limestone in this area is fossiliferous – indeed the limestone is made up from animals which died and fell to the sea bed where they form the fossils which subsequently were compressed to create the limestone rock more than 150 million years ago. The main road A419 is just to your left as you reach an information board and a narrow road. The board gives history of the canal junction and the Latton Basin, completed in 1819. Here is the junction point of the Thames-Severn canal and the North Wilts Canal which linked with the Wilts and Berks canal to the south (opened 1810). This link was abandoned in 1914, but restoration work began in 1998.

2. At a small stile by an old gate, you reach a narrow road, with a bridge over the main road to the left. Turn right here, and the driveway leads us to the former lock keeper's cottage, now a delightful modernised house and with a glorious garden. Pass to the left of this house and read another information board about the Wilts and Berkshire Canal. Go over a small footbridge and into the trees, where canal restoration work has been taking place. Follow the line of this canal to reach a gated footbridge. Once across the river, the path keeps straight ahead, but on the left is the entrance to North Meadow National Nature Reserve. This is one of the finest uncultivated ancient meadows in Britain, particularly famous for the large numbers of the rare snakeshead fritillaries to be seen in April or early May. During the summer, ladies bedstraw, meadowsweet and many other flowers appear, and a traditional cutting for hay takes place later in the year. If you wish, a circuit round this meadow would add a mile or so to the walk. But, your path leads straight ahead and soon reaches a bridge over the infant Thames – and here the circuit round North Meadow would rejoin our route. Turn right for our onward route, with the meandering Thames on your left. Reach a small stile by a gate and continue alongside the river on the left. Reach another stile and a gate, and the route of an old railway line (Gloucester-Swindon line built in 1883 and finally closed in 1960s).

3. Turn right here along a broad and straight track – a bridleway and also cycle track number 45. The Thames Path soon goes left but keep straight ahead, along the embanked track, with ditches on both sides. Numerous nesting boxes can be seen along here. A lake to your left is number 75 and on the right is a small pool with lawns and a house, just before passing beneath the narrow road. Cerney Wick is to the right along this road. Soon you reach a sign

with Cerney Wick to the right and straight ahead to South Cerney and Ashton Keynes. The track continues very straight as you walk on to pass the bittern sculpture (part of the Sculpture Trail) and then reach the main Spine Road by the old bridge and the Bridge Car park. Keep straight ahead, and the path passes some modern housing to the left of the path alongside lake number 16, and across lake 14 to your right is more modern housing. Once beyond the houses on the left, emerge onto the road leading into South Cerney (a Saxon parish – charter AD999), passing South Cerney Sailing Club.

4. A road turning sharp right, Wildmoorway Lane, leads to lakes 2 and 3, and can be used as a short cut if required. But, it is recommended to walk straight on along the main street in South Cerney – a very smart and tidy village, with many old Cotswold stone houses as well as modern developments – all in keeping with the environment. At the ancient cross turn right at Clarks Hay,

View towards South Cerney church

signed to Preston and Cirencester. Pass the Post Office and with Eliot Arms on the left, and the George Inn on the right, turn right along Bow Wow. This delightful narrow road runs between two river channels and is lined with flowers in the spring and early summer. Over to the left are several old Cotswold stone buildings including the church of All Hallows and the 17th century Atkins Manor with a stone gazebo by the river. When the road bends left cross the river and walk away from the last of the houses. Cross over the old railway bridge and reach a cross paths, with the footpath to Cirencester and golf course on the left and we turn right along the farm driveway to Crane Farm.

5. The footpath sign points to 'Cerney Wick 2m' and the old canal is now on your left. A canal information board gives more of the history of the Thames-Severn canal coming from Stroudwater canal (opened 1779) via the Sapperton Canal tunnel (1780-89) and explains why the Boxwell lock only has a drop of 3 ft 6 inches because of a small supply of water from a nearby spring. When the driveway bends right to the immaculate modernised buildings keep straight ahead (gate and stile – but the path sneaks round the gate). The path is slightly elevated, with the canal down to your left – and on the right is lake number 4. Pass an old lock and keep walking, then reach another lock and a renovated lock cottage. Here is a bridge over the canal, but keep ahead through two smart metal gates and soon the Cotswold Outdoor shop building comes into sight, and the Gateway Centre, as well as the traffic, on the Spine Road.

11. Hereford to Breinton

This route explores the centre of the town, starting from alongside the cathedral and the Mappa Mundi Museum, before following the banks of the tranquil Wye as far as the small hamlet of Breinton, returning to the city via fields and quiet country lanes.

Distance and time	7.5 miles; time required is 3-4 hours
Terrain	Very gentle and mostly flat. Paths are clear and firm though a short stretch alongside the river can be muddy in wet spells. The river bank may be flooded occasionally in winter
How to get there	On the A438 or A49 into the centre of Hereford. Parking in one of the town centre car parks – or alternatively, close to the church at Breinton (GR 472397)
Starting point	Near the Cathedral in Hereford: GR 508397
Refreshments	A large selection of pubs and cafés in Hereford
Tourist Information Centre	Hereford's Tourist Information Centre is close to the cathedral (01432 268430)
Other places of interest	In Hereford: the Cathedral, Mappa Mundi Museum and the Chained Library, the Cider Museum (01432 354207), Coningsby Medieval Museum and Chapel, housed in 13th century almshouses (01432 274049)
Maps	OS Landranger 149; Explorer 189

Hereford is not only a market town but also a cathedral city, playing host to the famous Three Choirs Festival every third year. Many ancient buildings still survive in the town centre. The Cathedral Church of St Mary the Virgin and St Ethelbert the King dominates the city centre, and parts of this ancient building date from 1079. Amongst its many attractions is the chained Library and the famous Mappa Mundi, a 13th century map of the world.

The walk

1. Adjacent to the Mappa Mundi Museum, at the end of Gwynne Street, where Nell Gwynne is thought to have been born, the walk begins through the town. From the Tourist Information Centre walk along Broad Street, with the Library, Museum and Art Gallery on the left. Opposite is the recently restored catholic church of St Francis Xavier with its Greek Doric columns. Notice the plaque on the wall of Barclays Bank and the reference to Nelson's visit here. This was formerly the City Arms, the site of the North Gate of the Saxon town and formerly the town house of the Duke of Norfolk. At the end of Broad Street is All Saints church, dating from the 13th century, and you turn right here to pass the Butter Market and reach High Town.

Plaque to the birth of Nell Gwynne, on Gwynne Street

The timber framed Old House at the east end of High Town was built in 1621, possibly as the home and shop of a Master Butcher. It was originally part of a row of buildings demolished in the 1830s. The interesting Museum inside this building is well worth a visit. Continue along St Peter's Street past the red sandstone St Peter's church with its graceful spire. The War Memorial stands in the middle of the road opposite the pillared Shire Hall. Next is the statue of Sir George Cornewall Lewis, with the quote of 'a wise and

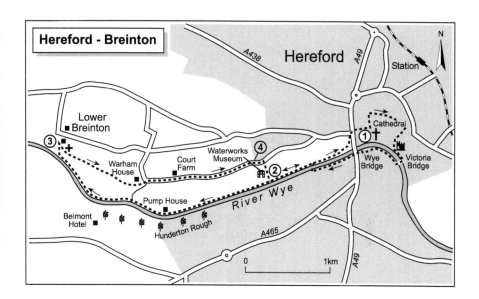

honest statesman', then walk on past the imposing Town Hall. The broad St Owen's Road is lined by many impressive Georgian buildings.

Turn right along St Ethelbert Street and at the Castle House turn right. Just past St Ethelbert's Hospital (dating from the 13th century) turn left along the footpath signed to the Castle Green and River Wye. Notice the rectangular pond, part of the original moat, and pass the Nelson Memorial of 1809 (with the quote 'and terminated a career of unexampled glory off Cape Trafalgar') on the way to the far left corner and the steps leading down to a narrow road. Cross over the Victoria Suspension Bridge dating from 1898, but restored and reopened in 2006, and turn right along the edge of Bishop's Meadow which extends away to our left. Walk along the riverside path, with good views to the cathedral and Bishop's Palace to reach the statue of the small dog and the plaque giving the story of its relevance to Elgar's *Enigma Variations*.

Walk up onto the six arched bridge. This old Wye bridge dates from 1490, was damaged in the Civil War and later widened in 1826. Go straight across St Martin's Street and continue along the

Old Wye Bridge

riverside path, soon passing beneath Greyfriars Bridge and the main road. The Hereford Rowing Club is based across the river and you walk on upstream towards Hunderton Bridge. This was the route of the old Great Western railway line, which carried trains from Hereford to Ross, and it now the route of Great Western Way, a green route and a cycle path. Beyond the bridge on a small hill can be seen the tower at the waterworks. Steps lead up onto the bridge and having crossed over the river, descend steps to reach the footpath leading upstream. Walk on, along the right side of the river (but called the left bank, because traditionally the expression left bank and right bank are based on going downstream). A surfaced path leads upstream, with the river to your left and playing fields of Hereford Cathedral School on the right – with some modern houses across on the other bank.

2. Reach a narrow road leading to the right, to the Waterworks Museum – well worth a visit but only open on Tuesdays and a few other selected days (phone 01432 344062). Containing hands-on models and very popular with school parties, the Museum tells the story of drinking water. Water was pumped from here up to the

reservoir higher on Broomy Hill. Between the river and the museum is Broomy Hill Junction and a small railway line – the location of the Hereford Society of Model Engineers.

Walking on upstream, follow the Wye Valley Way, now mud and grass rather than a surfaced path, and go on through a metal gate. This is Hereford Angling Club territory and you may notice numbered positions for fishermen to use. The riverside vegetation is home to many birds and can be noisy in spring and early summer with their song, including warblers and other summer visitors. You are now out of Hereford and into glorious countryside, with just a few houses across the river, well above flood level. Cross a gated footbridge over a small tributary stream and continue upstream on the narrow path, with a fence on your right with rich pastoral fields and cattle beyond. Walk on through a small metal gate and pass a river monitoring station, with the wooded slope of Hunderton Rough on the opposite bank. Continue along the river bank and over two gated footbridges and small streams. Wildflowers are numerous alongside the path, and a golf course is on the opposite bank. Go through a wooden kissing gate and cross a narrow field. Your onward route leads up the broad stony track, but first fork left for about 40 yards to visit the famous Breinton Spring, now almost hidden beneath shrubs and trees, but still flowing steadily.

Retrace steps to the stony track and climb up through the woods. Just before reaching a small National Trust car park, fork right through the old orchard to walk to the church of St Michael, mainly the work of Kempson 1866-1870, but a Norman window is one of the few remnants of the original church.

3. The route passes to the right of the church, through a metal kissing gate and along the path with the steep wooded slope going down to the right, and the Old Vicarage to the left. Wild flowers are abundant along this path in spring and early summer, and on the left is a large cider orchard. At the end of the orchard keep straight ahead through a wooden kissing gate. Walk along the field margin and look for the metal gate through the hedge. Once through the gate turn left to stay close to the hedge on the left margin of a narrow field. The river can be seen down to the right, and you pass

Warham House on the left, to reach a kissing gate and the narrow road. Turn right here and soon pass Warham Court with its stables. Many horses may be seen in the neighbouring fields. Good views open up across the river valley to the right and ahead to the hills beyond Hereford. Climb slightly to Broomy Hill where the outskirts of Hereford begin with houses which look across the river valley.

4. The entrance to the Waterworks Museum is on the right and this is also the entrance to the Hereford Society of Model Engineers (open on Sundays and occasional days each month), with the railway line seen earlier. Turn right here to walk back to the river bank (point 2) – and turn left, retracing steps as far as the Hunderton Bridge. Do not cross the river here, but stay on the left bank, with Hereford Rugby Club to your left. Continue towards the town, and at the Hereford Rowing Club the path turns left away from the river. This takes you out to a narrow road where you turn right, to reach a larger road, Barton Road, and St Nicholas' church where you turn right. Cross over the main road, with great care, and head straight along St Nicholas Street, which becomes King Street to arrive back at the Cathedral, the Tourist Information Centre and a choice of pubs, cafés and restaurants nearby.

Cathedral seen through the trees

12. Leintwardine

A gentle walk takes you on a circuit on the flat landscape close to the Teme-Clun confluence. As you cross the flower rich meadows, you can enjoy glorious views in all directions to the wooded hills which dominate in this very rural area.

Distance and time	About 4.5 miles – comfortably completed in 2 hours
Terrain	Gentle and mostly level – but can be wet underfoot in wet weather
How to get there	Along the A4113 west from Ludlow or A4110 north from Hereford
Starting point	Community Centre, Leintwardine alongside the main road – GR 403741
Refreshments	The recently refurbished Lion Hotel in Leintwardine (phone 01547 540203 – a very convenient alternative starting place – park here, with permission – walkers welcome) or the Walford Court Tea Room (01547 540570) on the A4113 between Leintwardine and Knighton
Tourist Information Centres	Knighton (01547 528753); Ludlow (01584 875053)
Other places of interest	Ludlow, Croft Castle, Wigmore Abbey ruins
Maps	OS Landranger 137; the walk starts on Explorer 203 but is mostly to be found on Explorer 201

Leintwardine was the important Roman settlement of Branogenium, though little evidence can be seen today. The Roman settlement continued to be occupied until the end of the 4th century AD, and the church is sited within the boundary of the Romano-British enclosure suggesting continued occupation of the area. Some of the town houses are of medieval origin, although there is no evidence of a market here. The present linear village extends northwards from the bridge over the River Teme. The tall tower of the sandstone St Mary Magdalene church is prominent. Built of local stone, with gravel coating it stands on the site of a Saxon church. The oldest parts date from 12th century and other parts are from 13th and 14th. Beneath the chancel is the location of part of the old Roman vallum which surrounded the settlement. Interesting features include the circular columns on the south side of nave – but octagonal on the other side. Notice the old clock with mechanism which dates back to the early 16th century, and alongside is an ancient bier, as well as an interesting historical exhibition of the local area. Impressive carved woodwork can be seen on the choir stalls, and wooden and stone carving near the altar. Round the corner to the north side of the altar is the North Chapel, with the rather hidden memorial to the remarkable Sir Banastre Tarleton Baronet who lived in Leintwardine from 1814-1833. Described as 'a tender husband, an indulgent Master and a liberal benefactor to the poor', but his reputation in USA was less complimentary because of his role in the American War of Independence. The well known film 'The Patriot' gave a slanted version of his activities.

The walk

1. From the community centre with its useful information board, and public toilets, walk back to the road, High Street (the original Watling Street). Turn right for a few yards, then left along Church Street. Visit the church, passing the notice board mentioning the wild life in the churchyard. There is also a swallow nesting in the porch. Continue along Church Street and at Watling Street turn right – passing a variety of houses including some delightful old cottages and colourful gardens. Amongst the larger houses is Watling House, with the carriage space incorporated in the house and a half timbered house next door – quite a mixture. Swifts, swallows and martins will be seen and heard overhead in early summer, and the gardens will be a blaze of colour. At the end of Watling Street, Rosemary Lane goes along to the left, with the Sun Inn and the Fish Bar along there, but you turn right. Pass the village green and good views of the bridge over the Teme. At the main

road turn right at the Lion Hotel with its attractive riverside garden. Pass the Post Office, then cross over to Mill Lane, the driveway between the buildings of the garage. The Post Office is on the site of the Roman Bath House. Walk along the narrow driveway Mill Lane, with houses on both sides. Pass the old mill on the left, and on the right is the entrance to Seedley House. Keep straight ahead, through an old metal gate, and just before the next gate, turn left over a stiled footbridge by a farm bridge, to cross over the River Clun.

2. Once across the river head straight across the field (your return route will come along the river from the right), skirt round any

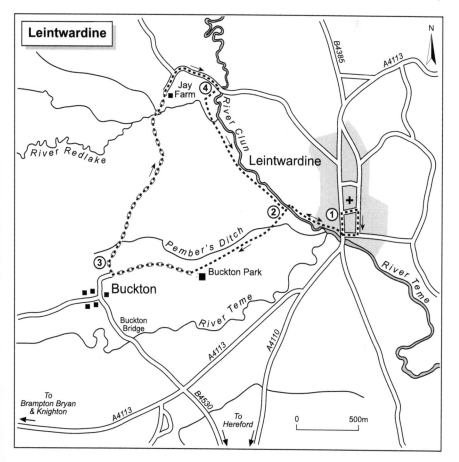

damp patches in this field
which will be covered with
buttercups in the early
summer. Ditches cross this
flat and damp landscape, but
the wooded Hopton and
Bucknell Hills can be seen
ahead and over to the right.
Cross a footbridge over the
ditch which runs along the
right margin of the next field.
The path does not stay close
to this ditch – named
Pember's. Head slightly right
from the stile, to follow
occasional single hawthorn
trees along the line of another
smaller and drier ditch. Over
to the right is the Pember's
and a line of large trees as
you cross this field, heading
towards the buildings of
Buckton Park. Go on over a
double stile and across a large
field with a line of large trees
and Pember's Ditch still 30-40
yards to the right. A few
patches of Ladies Smock in
this field suggest a few damp

Lion Hotel

Crossing the River Clun

patches. Go on over to stile to pass to the right of a huge old barn,
and walk through a small orchard. Keep ahead over the next stile
and along the track for 30 yards, which leads through to a narrow
road, with the buildings of Buckton Park to the left. Turn right.

3. Just before reaching the small village of Buckton, turn right along
    the track, between hedges. Many fields alongside the track are
    cropped, though one field on the right is very damp and covered
    with marsh vegetation including masses of yellow iris. Reach an
    iron gate across the track, but just continue ahead, and soon pass
    over a small stream with fish, damsel flies, and water crowfoot

flowers in the water. Look across to the left for views to Bedstone church and College building, with Hopton Hill beyond. Go on through another gate passing to the left of the buildings of Jay – and the attractive garden and pool. Walk on down the drive, to a narrow road, and at the junction fork right. Follow this road as it bends round to the right, with a drainage ditch alongside, and this leads round to the bridge over the River Clun.

4.   Just before the bridge go right, through a gate. There is a choice of paths here, but take the left option, close to the field margin. This winds across the field to a narrow footbridge and, once over this, turn left to cross the next field, moving closer to the River Clun, which is flowing along the left margin of this field. Pass more of the drainage ditches, which are vital in this watery landscape. Move slightly left through a gate and close to the riverbank. Stay close to the Clun and soon reach the bridge crossed earlier (at point number 2). Turn left over the stiled footbridge and then right along the track to retrace your steps into Leintwardine.

Old Bramley apple trees

13. Wapley Wood

Walking in this part of the Marches is to walk in Mortimer territory, named after the famous family who were so influential in this region. The route takes you through the woodland which clothes Wapley Hill, as you climb up to the Iron Age fort on the hill top where the views open out to look over the surrounding glorious countryside.

Distance and time	Nearly 4 miles; up to 2 hours, depending on how often you stop to look at birds, flowers, trees or the view
Terrain	Mostly good, wide and firm paths. Only two stiles and mostly gentle with only short steeper sections
How to get there	Along B4362 2 miles from Shobdon. Two narrow roads go off left at Byton, the first towards Pembridge but take the second signed to Wapley Hill Fort (following the brown sign). About a mile along here is the parking place and picnic spot. An Information Board describes a little about the management of the woods
Starting point	GR 358622
Refreshments	Pubs in Shobdon, Presteigne
Tourist Information Centre	Leominster (01568 616460)
Other places of interest	Shobdon church; black and white village of Pembridge
Maps	OS Explorer 201 or Landranger 149

Wapley Hill

An isolated hill though similar to other nearby hills such as Shobdon Hill dotted around these western margins of Herefordshire. Consisting of harder rocks than those surrounding, which is why they form hills, they have been slow to erode and remain upstanding above the general level of the countryside. The rocks are Ludlovian and Wenlock series from the Silurian period. Mostly forest-covered, the hill rises to over 1000 feet (379m – 1079 ft). The Iron Age fort is situated at the top and the hill is crossed by the Mortimer Trail, and many other footpaths and bridleways. The woods contain a variety of trees, and hence wild life, but includes areas of larch, Douglas fir and beech, as well as open areas and glades. Fifteen percent of the woodland will be returned to broadleaved species over the next 40 years. The top of the hill is open grassland, with the Iron Age fort having an internal area of 20 acres (8 hectares) and is surrounded by impressive ramparts and ditches. The north side of the fort is protected by a very steep and almost precipitous hillside. It is surrounded by up to four ditches and embankments, and the site is managed by English Heritage and the Forestry Commission – who ensure that the archaeological significance of the site is not threatened. The fort dates from 500 BC and the site was probably used in medieval times. Four quarries around the edges probably supplied the material for the embankments.

Roger Mortimer (1287-1330), descendant of a supporter of William the Conqueror, was the first of the family to be resident in this area. Wigmore castle was the main castle, but Ludlow was also used by the family, whose territory extended over much of Herefordshire and Shropshire and as far east as Cleobury Mortimer. Named after the important land owning family, the Mortimer Trail which follows the top of the ridge of Wapley Hill, is a 30 mile long distance path from Ludlow to Kington, climbing several small hills, passing through woodland and crossing the valleys of the Rivers Teme, Lugg and Arrow.

The walk

1. Walk back towards the entrance of the car park but before reaching the road turn left, along a broad stony track which climbs steadily. Birds, trees and flowers are abundant here in spring and summer. Ignore a left fork ,which is the route of your return, and stay on the main track. As this begins to level, a track and footpath go off to the right and turn here to follow the path, and the red

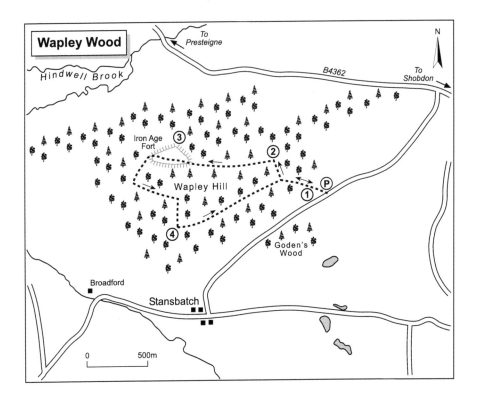

sign on a marker post. Walking through bluebells or crunching on beech mast, depending on the season, when the red marker posts point to the left, move to the right a few yards onto the track and continue climbing slightly. Reach a cross paths where you meet the Mortimer Trail and to the right is an open area with abundant wild flowers.

2. Turn left here along Mortimer Trail to follow the clear track through an avenue of fine coniferous trees. The undergrowth here is mainly brambles and bracken. The going is nearly level along this stretch, just climbing slightly. Reach a cross paths by a smart wooden seat, where red marked post route goes left, and red route and the Mortimer Trail goes right. Go right, into dark fir trees, following a green logo of Mortimer Trail, and soon reach an open area – the site of the old Iron Age fort. Climb over the stile to walk into the fort, with the impressive and well preserved embankments

Ramparts to the Iron Age fort

and ditches and then a large grassy flat area with scattered trees. Bird noises are likely to serenade you here in spring or summer, with warblers and tree pipits in fine voice. The good views all around take in the Black Mountains and Hay Bluff.

3. The Mortimer Trail turned left just before the stile leading into the fort, but keep straight ahead through the fort heading in a westerly direction and still following the red route markers. At the end of the fort drop down quite steeply, with a boundary wall on your right. Go over the stile and continue to descend, and as the path levels it divides (straight ahead and descending, or turning left). Turn left here, still following the red marks on the posts. Climb slightly along a clear track through an area of beech trees, heading in an easterly direction and still following the marked red circular walk. A track goes off to the left, but keep straight ahead to soon reach a cross-tracks. The Mortimer Trail comes down from the left, near Warren House, and goes on to the right, as does the red route.

Turn right here, following the red circle, yellow arrow and green shield, and descend steadily through an area of fine beech trees – with larch over to the right.

4. At a cross-tracks by another very smart bench, turn left following the red marker. Follow this broad track as far as a narrow path shown by a red marker, leading off to the right into the woods. This winds through the trees and there may be muddy patches, as you approach the edge of the woods, and areas with masses of bluebells. Good views open up across the surrounding countryside, as the path undulates up and down through the trees. When you reach a cross-track, we keep straight ahead and soon reach the stony track where you walked earlier. Turn right here and retrace steps to the car park.

View to Wales from the west end of the fort

14. Croft Castle and Croft Ambrey

Set in the heart of beautiful Borders countryside, Croft Castle stands in parkland sloping up to the hill top where the Iron Age camp of Croft Ambrey is situated. Partially wooded, the hill is the setting for a glorious walk, with all round views from the grassy summit.

Distance and time	4 miles – about 2 hours. Additional signed walks can be followed around the park
Terrain	A short climb up to the fort and then a descent down but otherwise fairly gentle. Paths clear and fairly dry, although muddy patches may be encountered in the woods
How to get there	Along the A4110 Hereford to Knighton road, turn right at Mortimer's Cross along B4362 and follow the signs to Croft Castle
Starting point	In the car park (payment required for non members of the National Trust) at Croft Castle. GR 452657
Refreshments	Croft Castle when it is open (phone 01568 780246 – from March to November). Otherwise the nearest food is the good pub at Mortimer's Cross
Tourist Information Centre	Leominster (phone 01568 616460)
Other places of interest	Shobdon church with its unusual Strawberry Hill Gothic design, and blue and white interior; Wigmore Castle ruins
Maps	OS Landranger 149; Explorer 203

Croft Castle is a late 17th century castellated stone Manor House, noted for its Georgian interiors, and a recently restored walled garden containing many unusual plants, a vineyard and an orchard of old varieties of Herefordshire apples. House and garden are surrounded by 630 hectares of parkland, and a total estate of more than 1500 acres. There are over 300 veteran trees in the park, and new young trees have recently been planted. The Croft family has been connected with the house for 1000 years, although some of the management was handed to the National Trust in 1957. The adjacent church of St Michael's dates from about 1300, and is open to visitors.

Croft Castle from the entrance drive

The Iron Age fort of Croft Ambrey is located on the hill top at nearly 1000 ft above sea level. The northern edge stands on the top of a very steep slope and ramparts and ditches line the south and western edges of the fort. Evidence has been found of about 300 dwellings, with rows of houses and streets. Research has revealed signs of human occupancy from 6th century BC up till AD48, and there is archaeological evidence of grain and animals as well as remnants of weaving.

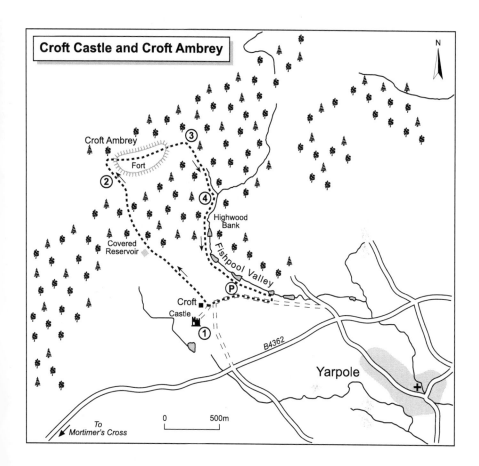

The walk

1. Start from the car park near the castle – payment is necessary for
    non members of the National Trust. Walk through the kissing gate
    by the large metal gate between the car park and the Carpenters Tea
    Room. A blue arrow points the way. Follow the surfaced drive as it
    begins to wind uphill. Soon reach the sign saying 'Footpath to Croft
    Ambrey' and then pass a small house on the left. The surfaced drive
    becomes a muddy track as you climb up to a stile by a metal gate.
    The stile has the very useful tall pole that acts as a handle. Pass the
    two very old Spanish chestnuts where a notice gives information
    about the significance of the trees and mentions one which is

included in the list of *50 Great British Trees*. Continue along the right side of an open stretch of parkland, with views across to Hay Bluff and Brecon Beacons. Slightly to the left is an avenue of mature trees and also several young trees, planning for future generations. Climb gently up the hill and, on your left, the small mound is a covered reservoir. Reach a small wooden kissing gate by a large gate and keep straight ahead, into the woods. Follow the sign to Croft Ambrey, pass the Forestry Commission sign and climb steadily along the broad stony track. The trees are mainly coniferous here, with a line of deciduous lining the track – and a carpet of bluebells in the spring. At a cross tracks continue straight ahead, passing a Croft Wood notice board with information about land management, including pollarding and double decker land use. Climb steadily, and soon reach the Croft Castle National Trust Information Board on our right.

2. Continue along a grassy track, which descends to a gate with a long handled stile alongside. The blue arrow points right, but fork slightly left and follow the main track. The path narrows and can be muddy, and the land slopes steeply down to the left here. Continue along the path, which winds a little – but soon leave this path to go over a stile to the right. This leads to a broad path which climbs steadily up into the fort. The clear path climbs up to the top of the hill, through grass, bracken and scattered trees. Cross the open summit and this is the area where evidence of small houses has been found. Birds including tree pipits will be singing in spring and summer – and throughout this walk a variety of birds can be seen. Binoculars will be invaluable for enjoying the birds as well as admiring the surrounding views. Views open up to the north, looking straight out to the buildings of Hall Farm and beyond is the massive scar of Leinthall Earls Quarry. Follow the clear path along the edge of the fort, with the very steep slope (easily defended) down to your left. The spring, which provided water for the inhabitants, is just down to the left on this steep slope.

3. The path begins to descend quite steeply, past an embankment, and then a very old yew tree, to reach a fence with a stile. Over here turn right, and after a few yards, before the straight ahead path begins to climb, turn right through a wooden gate, and begin to descend, following the Mortimer Trail and a yellow arrow. Descend to a cross paths and a major track, but keep straight

One of the 50 Great British trees

ahead along a narrow path signed circular walk and Mortimer Trail. After another 50 yards reach a cross track but still keep straight ahead on the Mortimer Trail.

4. Descend to the main valley where you turn right along a clear track (Mortimer Trail and Circular Walk). You are now in Fishpool Valley, which was extensively re-landscaped in about 1780. Medieval fish ponds were restored and Gothic structures created. The valley contains seven pools in 80 acres of woodland, and part has been designated a Site of Special Scientific Interest (SSSI). Reach the first pool, surrounded by very lush vegetation, and on the right is the stone grotto, and soon on your left, is the old pumping house. This is a grade II listed building and dates from early 19th century. Carry on along the path, ignoring the track going left across a small dam, then bend slightly right and, after 20 yards, the track divides. The left fork here is Mortimer Trail, but leave the valley and the pools by forking right and passing rhododendron bushes. Climbing quite steeply, reach the main driveway where you turn right to walk back into the parking area and the castle.

View across towards Clee Hill

15. Titley

The first part of this walk leads to the church and then along Mortimer Trail through farmland to a hill top farm. You then proceed along the ridge before descending back to Titley, and complete the walk with a visit to Titley Pool. Beautiful scenery and wonderful all round views make this gentle walk a pleasure at any time of the year.

Distance and time	6 miles – time required about 3 hours
Terrain	Includes a steady climb from the church and ends with a descent back into the village. Some paths may be muddy in wet weather
How to get there	Along the B4355, 3 miles north east of Kington
Starting point	At the Stagg Inn (with permission – phone 01544 230221) or Village Hall in Titley, GR 329597
Refreshments	A very good pub in Titley
Tourist Information Centre	Kington (01544 230778)
Other places of interest	Black and white villages in Pembridge and Eardisland; the small towns of Kington and Presteigne
Maps	OS Landranger 148; or Explorer 201

Titley is situated in the Arrow Valley, but above flood level, and close to Offa's Dyke. There has been a settlement here since ancient times, including a small Priory close to the present church. Dating from 1120, the priory was linked with the Benedictine Abbey at Tiron in La Beauce, and remnants of earthworks and fishponds can be seen on the edge of Priory Wood. The present church of St Peter's dates from 1868, and inside can be seen the remarkable story of Lazar Meszaros, a Hungarian General whose grave is in the churchyard. He successfully led the Hungarian Army against the Austrians, then later fled to Turkey, Britain and eventually USA, but whilst visiting friends at Eywood House was taken ill and died here, in 1858.

Titley Pool, half a mile from the village is now managed by Herefordshire Nature Trust (01432 356872). It is home to a wide range of birds which can be watched from the small hide on the southern side of the lake. The origin of the lake, and several others nearby, is in a kettle hole. This is the result of a block of ice being deposited with tons of clay and rocks dumped by a retreating ice sheet or glacier at the end of the Ice Age about 10,000-11,000 years ago. As the block of ice melted a hollow formed and was subsequently filled with water.

The walk

1. The Stagg was formerly know as the Balance Inn, and has had a varied and sometimes chequered history. A previous owner, the Greenleys of Titley Court, closed the pub for several years because the railway workers from Titley Junction became too drunk on Sundays. Nowadays it has a fine reputation for wonderful food and attracts customers from a wide area.

The Stagg Inn

Leave the car park and turn left along the road. Soon pass a few houses, including the grand Titley House on the right, opposite the sandstone War Memorial. Just before reaching the church, on the left is the old well, presented by Louisa Elizabeth Lady Hastings of Eywood House, in 1864. Formerly a pipe linked the 14th century stoup at the Priory with this roadside drinking well. Next on the left is the church of St Peter, with the Old Vicarage on the opposite side of the road. The Old Vicarage has a large garden which supplies food to the Stagg. The short tower of the church is at the west end and the roof of the main

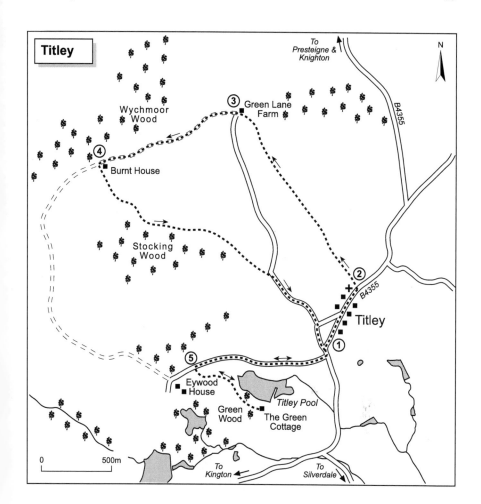

part of the church is at two levels. Solid pillars on the north side support the nave and on the north wall is a memorial article about Lieutenant-General Lazar Meszaros, supreme Commander of the Hungarian Army (1848-49). Just past the church turn left along a stony track, signed Mortimer Trail. Pass the east end of the church with its unusual supporting buttresses.

2. Keep straight ahead on a broad path climbing up the edge of the field. As you look back for views of the church, note the small wood, Priory Wood – at the western edge of which are the remnants

of earthworks. At the top of the large field keep straight ahead through a gap in the hedge, and walk on the right margin of another large field. Enjoy the all round views from here. Looking to the south east can be seen the small pointed Pyon Hill and beyond is the ridge of the Malvern Hills. Continue straight ahead across two fields and over two stiles, and then head just to the right of the buildings of Green Lane Farm. Here a yellow arrow points through the farmyard, but follow the sign for Mortimer Trail and Circular Walk over a stile to the right of the farmyard gate. Wonderful views open towards the north east, and Wapley Hill.

3. Stay near the left margin of this small field to reach a stile beyond which you turn left for a few yards. With the farm to your left, turn right along the broad level track - still on Mortimer Trail. The very smart stone house Wychmoor, and its large modern barns, will be on the right as you keep ahead along the Green Lane - an old ridge top route probably dating back for thousands of years, linking Wales with the Marches. Pass through a large metal gate and continue along the broad track lined by trees, mainly hazel, which

View towards Hay Bluff

show signs of coppicing in the past. Continue beyond a stile by a gate and soon reach a magnificent old barn – named Burnt House. Note the large door for carts and perhaps a former living area at the end.

4. Just past the building, and before the gate and stile, turn left following the sign to Titley. Descend along a sunken lane, with overhanging trees making an archway, and emerge into more open country. Descend down to the right to the bottom of the valley. Turn left along the valley floor to a gap in the fence and then a stile located near the right hand end of a hedge on the next field boundary. The trees of Stocking Wood are just 50 yards to your right here, and many of the trees are deciduous and have been planted to replace the coniferous trees in many parts of the wood. The path leads more or less straight ahead, to reach a track, then a stony drive and out to a narrow road. Turn right, pass a few houses, then the Village Hall on your left – with a large parking area, and climb slightly up to reach the main road, at point number 1. The pub is to your left, but turn right for the continuation of the walk to Titley Pool. After a few yards turn right again, along the narrow road signed to Eywood Lane. Pass the Lodge House on the left and the magnificent stone and wood Balance Barns on the right. The road leads between fields in the glorious countryside, and the pool soon becomes visible through trees to the left.

5. About half a mile along this narrow road, by an old tumbledown shed in the field on the left, leave the road to walk along a stony track through the woods. Turn left at a large metal gate and follow a stony-grassy track across a large open field. This leads to a wooden gate with a notice saying 'Welcome to Titley Pool Nature Reserve' – a Herefordshire Nature Trust notice. The track continues ahead but fork right along a narrow path signed 'Nature Trail'. The path stays close to the right edge of the woods at first and then bends slightly left. Reach a fence and walk alongside this for a short distance, still following the clearly marked path, to reach an information board which tells you this is one of the largest areas of open water in Herefordshire. The undulating countryside around here is the result of kettle moraine, clay sand and gravel dumped as the ice melted. Amongst the wild life which may be seen here are many summer visitor birds including

warblers, pied flycatcher and redstart, as well as all the water birds ducks, geese, swans, grebes, coots and herons and occasionally the very shy and elusive water rail. The wood is a remnant of a very ancient woodland, and is carpeted by bluebells in the spring. Walk on from the information board, cross a track, where the house, The Green, is a few yards to the right. Keep ahead as the path leads down to the Pool. Turn left here for a few yards to reach the hide. From the hide the path continues alongside the pool and then bends left to return to the wooden gate, and the large open field. As you cross the field notice ahead, and to the left, the fine old Eywood House. Retrace steps through the wood and out to point number 5, and along the narrow road back to Titley.

Titley church

16. Eardisley

This walk in the Welsh Marches takes you through the delightful black and white village of Eardisley, across Eardisley Park with stunning all round views and visits a remarkable ancient oak tree and an equally old man-made feature, the font in the church of St Mary Magdalene.

Distance and time	5 miles, or short cut route of 3.5 miles – 2-3 hours
Terrain	An easy level or gently undulating walk mostly on tracks and country lanes
How to get there	Take the A438 road from Hereford to Hay-on-Wye, and turn right along the A4111 towards Kington.
Starting point	Close to the church: GR 312492
Refreshments	Pub, restaurant and tea shop in the village
Tourist Information Centres	Kington (phone number 01544 230778); Hay-on-Wye (phone 01497 820144)
Other places of interest	Hay-on-Wye and its bookshops; Kinnersley two miles to the east: the black and white village of Weobley
Maps	OS Explorer 201; Landranger 148

The church of St Mary Magdalene dates from the 12th century, with additions in 13th and 14th. The tower was built in 1708 to replace an earlier wooden structure. The interior holds many notable features but outstanding is the 12th century font, a product of the Herefordshire School, and still in remarkably good condition. The carvings tell stories including a scene of Knights fighting and a scene of Christ with a Dove on his shoulder. The Baskervilles were the Lords of the Manor from 1066 for 500 years, and their home was Eardisley Castle. Only a mound remains from their castle (in the grounds of Castle Farm, an 18th century brick building to the west of the church) but they do have memorials in the church. Memorials can also be seen to the Barnsley family who succeeded the Baskervilles as Lords of the Manor. They fought a 34 year long legal battle in the 18th century, which was very costly, and perhaps was used as the basis for the Jarndyce versus Jarndyce legal wrangles used by Charles Dickens in *Bleak House.*

Tram Square was probably the original market area of the village, where the local shepherds and labourers would be hired. The name is taken from the tramway which linked Brecon to Eardisley and subsequently to Kington. It reached Eardisley in 1818, but the tramway never passed the Tram Inn. However, the inn was used as stables for the horses which pulled the trucks on the tramway. Coal was the main cargo heading north, and stone the main cargo going south.

The walk

1. Walk alongside the church, following the narrow roadway. As this bends left, it is worth making the detour to visit the church, with its remarkable font. The driveway bends right once past the church, and soon on the left is Eardisley Castle Millennium Green, with a small orchard, and children's playground. On the right, in the woods is a rookery, noisy in spring, and the site of the old castle, the home of the Baskervilles. Emerge into open country, with views all around – especially towards the left, with Merbach Hill and the northern edge of the Black Mountains near Hay-on-Wye in the distance. Just beyond a house and barn a path goes off to the left, towards Winforton, but keep ahead along the straight track.

2. SHORT CUT OPTION: When the track bends slightly to the right, before reaching the grand house seen ahead, look for a stile and footpath sign to the right. Turn here, and cross the middle of the large field close to the lone oak tree and head for the right corner of the field to reach a stile by a large metal gate. Follow the right margin of the field to a small wooden gate, along the edge of the next small field to a footbridge. Go along the edge of the next field

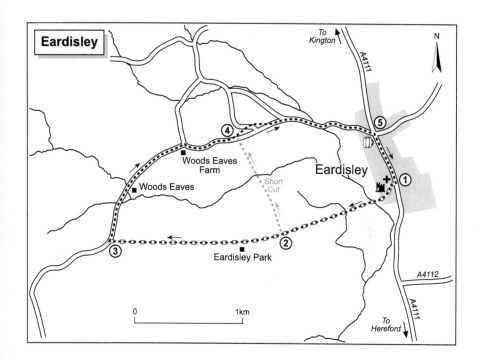

to reach a small white cottage and a driveway. The driveway leads between the avenue of trees and slightly uphill to a narrow road at point 4 – turn right here to rejoin the main route.

The main route keeps straight ahead, climbing slightly as you pass the fine Eardisley Park house with barns and stables. The track leads on between two delightful houses where the metalled surface ends. Walk through the gate and along the field margin, still following a clear track. This leads to a narrow road, and a lone house, Red Gates, with Cattery and Boarding Kennels.

3. Turn right along this narrow road to walk through the small village of Woods Eaves, with several very attractive gardens. Next pass a few more houses and Woods Eaves Farm, before reaching the point where the short cut route comes up from the right.

4. Walk on for about 150 yards, enjoying the views to several wooded hills including Garnons and Burton over to the right, to reach the

Ducks on the stream in Woodeaves

Old Manse. Turn left by the Old Manse to visit the remarkable old tree, the Great Oak, with a hollow interior, and still thriving although more than 800 years old. The oak is possibly a remnant of the Hurstway Forest, which was mentioned in the Domesday Book. Beyond here walk on along the signed footpath (Herefordshire Trail), passing a few old gravestones and then along a narrow path between fences, to a stile and a small field. Stay close to the left margin of two fields to reach a stile and gate, and a narrow road. Turn left here for a few yards then go right over a stile, and turn right to walk close to the hedge. At the end of this large narrow field reach a stile and a large gate, and return to the road. Turn left here and walk back into the village, passing Chennels Gate Nursery on the right. Just before crossing a small bridge, notice, but ignore, the footpath going right, unless wishing to take a short cut. This path leads across fields to the site of the castle near the church and your starting point. But keep ahead into the village, passing between the first of the black and white buildings and the old Eardisley village pump in a small brick shelter. Reach the main road by The Tram, and the location of the former Tram Square – now on a busy main road. On the opposite side of the road is The New Strand (phone 01544 327285), bookshop, restaurant, café with home made cakes – and also the Post office.

5. Walk through the village, passing several old black and white houses, and the Village Hall reached through an archway. As you approach the church, notice the large black and white buildings on the right, former barns now private residences in Castle Close. As you return to the church to complete the circuit, notice the village school on the left. The school was founded in 1857 by the Lord of the Manor Mr William Perry-Herrick.

The Great Oak

17. Brockhampton

A circular route round the estate through farmland, park and woods, with abundant birds and animals. Walks around the park were first opened up in 1971.

Distance and time	5½ miles. Time requirement 2-3 hours. With an extension to Bromyard Down the distance would become 8 miles in 3-4 hours
Terrain	Undulating and quite steep in places, with some muddy patches
How to get there	From the A44 Bromyard to Worcester road, 2 miles east of Bromyard, turn left off the main road follow driveway signed to Lower Brockhampton, and park close to the café in a large car parking area
Starting point	GR 684549
Refreshments	Apple Tree café in the car park (open daily in summer from 10-5; Wednesday to Sunday in spring and summer; weekends in winter – phone 01885 488099); choice of pubs and cafés in Bromyard
Tourist Information Centre	Bromyard (01432 260280)
Other places of interest	Bromyard Down, Bringsty Common
Maps	OS Explorer 202; Landranger 149

Brockhampton Estate was acquired by the National Trust in 1946. There is still a Brockhampton House – but it is private. The National

Trust owns Lower Brockhampton, described as a romantic moated manor house – in an idyllic setting. Ruins of a Norman chapel still survive in the farmyard just to the west of the house. The chapel was probably built by the Brockhampton family about 1180. The present house is thought to date from about 1400 and was built by John Domulton, a descendant of the Brockhampton family. It is surrounded by a moat which may have been a fishpond as well as a useful defensive protection. Animals could be brought inside if necessary. The Great Hall was built by the estate carpenters, using timbers from fine oak trees growing on the estate. A large east wing consists of two storeys and there had possibly been a west wing sometime in the past. The Gatehouse dates from about 1500 and it too consists of two storeys. Built straddling the moat it is very picturesque and photogenic. Between the small car park and entrance way to Lower Brockhampton and the Gatehouse and pond is a small damson orchard, which is noted for the damson jam on sale here in the autumn.

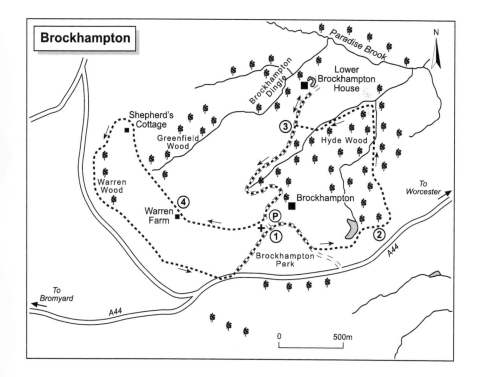

The walk

1. From the main car parking area in a former walled garden, walk out to the drive way following the signs to the walks – you are following the green Oak walk. Other shorter walks are the Ash, Holly, Beech. Pass the small stone Gothic chapel (dates from 1798), and once beyond the cattle grid turn left following yellow and green arrows across the grass. Go on over a stile and across grass and through the parkland – with wonderful

Carved wooden archway

views opening up to the left. Descend quite steeply and cross a driveway. Over to the left, catch a glimpse of Brockhampton House. Continue to descend, past a lone Wellingtonia to reach a wooden stile by a wooden gate. Just before the stile is the stone and brick remnant of an apple press, a relic of the days when there were apple orchards on this slope.

2. Continue to another stile and then the path divides, with Lawn Pool to the left. This small lake was created as a landscape feature but is now home to fish, birds and frogs. Take the right fork, and begin to climb up into the wood. The zig-zag path climbs up quite steeply and at the top the path forks and you go left, following green, red and blue markers. Look out for the wooden cartwheel shape picnic table on the left. The path forks again where you go left, to reach the Holybank car park. Walk on and fork right when the path next divides and pass beneath the carved wooden archway. Follow the green markers (the red turns left – but ignore that). Reach a very steep descent, some of which is stepped and with a rail, to cross a small stream and then climb up the other side of the valley. Keep straight ahead and climb gradually to a major crossing point of four broad tracks, where you turn right. At a T-junction turn left and soon join a broader stonier track where

you turn right. Cross a small stream and the track bends round to the left and begins to climb again.

3. Reach a narrow surfaced road – the route back to the starting point goes left here – but first turn right to visit Lower Brockhampton House. This idyllic house is well worth a visit (you can drive from the car park if you wish), and after looking round the house, gatehouse and farm yard displays, retrace steps along the driveway to point number 3. Walk steadily uphill through the woods and, at the cattle grid, emerge into the open grassland which sweeps up through the park. Pass the entrance to Brockhampton Mews, the modern house, which would have been seen to your left in the early part of the walk, and then the Walled Garden house – both private. Arrive back at the car park, toilets, award winning Apple Store Tea Room, with the *Cycle of Life* sculpture in the garden.

Lower Brockhampton Gatehouse

If further walking is desired an interesting extension can take you over to the top of Bromyard Down. To start on this extension return to the driveway to Lower Brockhampton but turn left to follow the signs to 'Estate Office and Greenfield Cottages'. After 70-80 yards, as the driveway bends right, keep straight ahead along a track across the field containing several magnificent old gnarled oaks – which may be 500 years old. Continue along the track between fence and hedge, climbing gently up to Warren Farm which offers a farm shop, tea room and farm visits.

4. Turn right past the farm complex and keep straight ahead along a track. Reach Shepherd's Pool and a small gate onto a footpath, which leads to the shepherd's cottage with a collection of amazing objets d'art in the garden. Pass through the garden to the top of Bromyard Down and turn left towards the woods. The grassy slope down to the right has been the location of a golf course and a race course in the past. Enter Warren Woods by a stile with a tall handle, and fork right to follow the path through the woods. Stay close to the right margin of the woods passing a small gate on the right. At the second gate on the right, by the National Trust sign for Brockhampton. Leave the woods through the kissing gate and turn left along the top of the common. Stay close to the edge of the common and, when it begins to descend, turn left over a stile. Walk along the left margin of the field to reach a driveway where you keep straight ahead to the main road A44. Turn left along the verge as far as the entrance to Brockhampton Estate and walk along the drive, passing the Lodge House before reaching the small church and the car park area.

18. Cat's Back on Black Hill

Black Hill, also known as Crib-y-Garth, is the most easterly ridge of the Black Mountains, reaching up to a height of 640m, the highest point of Herefordshire and also the highest point in England south of Yorkshire. The knife edged Cat's Back is the southerly end of the ridge. The walk starts from the car park and climbs gradually up the beautiful green Olchon valley, with high hills on both sides. The peace and quiet are most noticeable in this isolated spot, where the greatest noises are likely to be the wind and, in spring and early summer, the sheep and lambs. After reaching the top of the valley turn to walk along the broad ridge top of Black Hill to reach the dramatic landscape of Cat's Back with all round views, east and south across Herefordshire and west into Wales and the Brecon Beacons.

Distance and time	
Terrain	After a short descent from the car park, the gentle climb up the valley is along narrow road then clear track which becomes rocky towards the top of the climb. Easy walking along the ridge and then sections of rocky path for the final descent from the Cat's Back
How to get there	Leave the A465 Hereford to Abergavenny road at Pontrilas and take the B4347 to Ewyas Harold. The road narrows to follow the minor road signed to Dulas and Longtown. Descend into the village, to turn right at the pub. Pass Longtown castle and follow signs to Llanveynoe and then to the Black Hill Picnic Place. The narrow road leads up into the car park, at a height of 400m
Starting point	Black Hill Picnic site – GR 288328

Refreshments	Crown Inn in Longtown (01873 860217); Bull's Head in Craswall (01981 510616)
Tourist Information Centres	Abergavenny (01873 857 588) and Hay-on-Wye (01497 820144)
Other places of interest	Hay-on-Wye and its bookshops, Abbey Dore and Abergavenny
Maps	OS Outdoor Leisure 13; Landranger 161

The Black Mountains mainly consist of rocks from the Old Red Sandstone geological period, dating from about 400 million years ago. As the name suggests many of the rocks are sandstone, some of which are very hard. This explains the formation of the steep hills, as the rocks resist erosion. The land on either side of the Black Hill ridge has been worn away by rivers over millions of years, with assistance from ice during the Ice Age.

The walk

1. A useful information board stands in the car park, telling us of some of the attractions, including heather and the varied bird life such as grouse and merlin. But there are many other birds to be seen as well, perhaps wheatear, ring ouzel, and numerous pipits and skylarks. There are also warnings about inclement weather and the rocky landscape – so take care on this walk, and be prepared for a sudden change in weather conditions.

    Over the stile is the route to Cat's Back, but you are not going that way. Turn round and walk back down the road as far as the T-junction where you turn right. Enjoy the wonderful views of hills all around, as you walk along the road, in a typical mid-Wales upland landscape, even though you are just in Herefordshire. The county and national boundary runs along the top of Hatterall ridge the our left, which is not only the boundary but is also the route of Offa's Dyke Long Distance footpath. At first the route is fairly level along the valley, with green fields on both sides, passing a very smart stone house and then several old abandoned stone houses – evidence of former occupants having left this isolated area.

2. Climb slightly and just before the road goes down quite steeply towards the river bridge, fork right off the road to follow an old sunken track, signed bridleway. This wide stone and mud track is lined with trees, and many wild flowers on the banks. Bird song will be noisy in the springtime. Climb steadily to reach a metal gate and continue straight ahead, now reaching more open country,

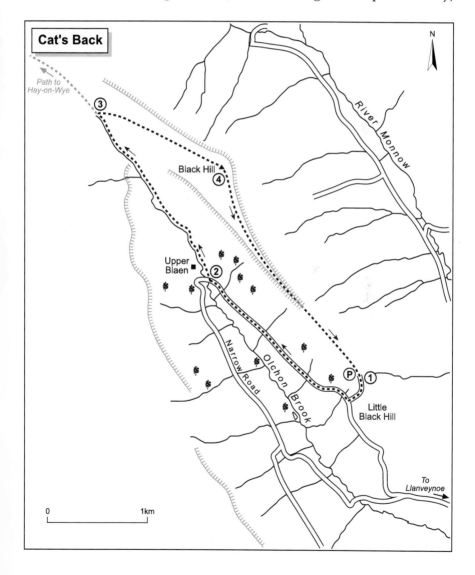

Narrow ridge of Cat's Back, towards the end of the walk

with a few trees on your left. Cross several small streams draining into the river down to the left. This river is the Olchon, a tributary of the River Monnow. The fence turns left but keep straight ahead on the open landscape, with large areas of bilberry in this area. Look out for the varied bird life as well as the wild horses which search for suitable food for grazing in this area. Climb steadily and reach a steeper section where the valley narrows. A rocky path leads out at the top end of the valley and the path becomes nearly horizontal, with a small stream to the left.

3. The clear broad path reaches a T-junction and a small rock cairn. Hay-on-Wye is to the left, but turn right along the wide track. Now on the flat top of the ridge, begin to walk in a south easterly direction. Good views open up across to the right, over the Olchon Valley to Hatterall Ridge and into Wales. As you progress views also open up to the left into Herefordshire, with a pattern of small fields down in the valley. The triangulation point is visible on the

skyline half a mile ahead. Much of the ridge top is covered with heather, although the path is both grassy and rocky in places, with occasional small pools where impeded drainage has left waterlogged ground.

4. Reach the triangulation point at 640m and enjoy the all round views. It is difficult to imagine any better viewpoint. Much of Herefordshire can be seen over to the east, together with some of Gloucestershire and even the Shropshire Hills. Malvern Hills, Bredon, May Hill, Clee Hill and even the Mendips and Caer Caradoc are visible on a clear day. To the west is Wales with the Brecon Beacons just showing above Hatterall ridge. Keep straight ahead and begin a slight descent, to reach the narrow ridge of the Cat's Back. Rocky outcrops increase – often with horizontal slabs of the sandstone rock which has created this steep sided ridge. The path descends steadily, over a series of large rocky steps and the ridge narrows – this is Cat's Back. At the final rocky outcrop the grassy slope ahead comes into view and you descend steeply to the car park.

Triangulation point on top of Black Hill, with Hatterall ridge beyond

19. Garway

In the stunning scenery of this beautiful rural area, where the River Monnow has cut a path through the hills, walk along country lanes and across meadows where sheep are peacefully grazing, as well as visiting a remarkable church.

Distance and time	5 miles – 2-3 hours depending on time spent in the church or churches
Terrain	Along country lanes and across fields, descending during the first half of the walk then climbing steadily in the second half
How to get there	From Ross bypass take the A49 Hereford road and after about 3 miles turn left along the B4521 towards Abergavenny. Cross the A4137 at Owen's Cross where there is a good pub (The New Inn – phone 01989 730274), then cross the A466 and after a further mile turn right at the cross roads in Broad Oak. This leads to Garway and the starting point at the The Moon inn (with permission – phone 01600 750270) or on the edge of the Common
Starting point	On the Common at Garway: GR 465227
Refreshments	Local pubs in Garway (not open every lunch time in mid week), Skenfrith (closed on Tuesdays); and Owen's Cross
Tourist Information Centre	Ross-on-Wye (phone 01989 562768)
Other places of interest	Grosmont castle, Kilpeck church, How Caple Gardens and Ross-on-Wye
Maps	OS Landranger 161; Explorer 189

Garway church

Although there is evidence for an earlier church on this site, the church of St Michael was founded between 1165 and 1168. The Manor of Garway was owned from the 12th to 16th centuries by the Knights Templars and the Knights Hospitallers. The Templars built St Michael's church in their traditional style with a round nave and square chancel, just like the Temple church in London. The round nave was probably an imitation of the Church of the Holy Sepulchre in Jerusalem. When the Order of Knights Templars was accused of heresy and disbanded by Pope Clement V in 1312 (although they have recently received an apology from the Vatican) the Manor of Garway was given to the Knights of St John, the Hospitallers, who owned it until the dissolution of the monasteries in the 16th century. The present nave was built in the 15th century as the round nave was difficult to repair. The square tower was built separately in the 13th century and was used as a refuge from marauding invaders from the west. The tower was connected to the nave more than 300 years ago.

Garway stone church

The walk

1. Walk on along the road, passing the school on the right and the village hall on the left. Ignore a walk going left and then a walk going right, pass the right turn signed to 'Garway Hill and Bagwyllydiart' and keep ahead towards Pontrilas. Going downhill, after about 100 yards go left through an old iron kissing gate and head diagonally right across the field towards the church – the rooftop is just showing across the field. A small gate leads into the churchyard and the amazing little stone church, one of only six churches built in England by the Templars. On returning from the Holy Land many Crusaders built churches and copied the circular architecture they had seen and admired. Inside the church the

14th century rectangular nave replaced the original 12th century round nave, and the very solid pews are from the 16th and 17th centuries. At the far end of the nave is the wonderful chancel arch with the Norman zig-zag carvings which are edged by the waterleaf capitals, rare in Herefordshire churches, and possibly a design copied from the Far East. Features in the South Chapel include an ancient oak chest, the piscina in the south wall, and in the east wall is an aumbrey, or cupboard, for the communion dishes.

Skenfrith church

Also, there is much to see in the churchyard, including a healing garden close to the ancient well. The Holy Well is an ancient spring which flowed until the mid 1970s. It formerly fed two fish ponds lower down the valley, which dated from the time of the Knights Templar in the 12th century – and were used by the Knights Hospitallers, their successors. It also provided a water supply for the village, which was in use until the 1950s. The church was built in this location because the spring provided water for baptisms. Walking along the north side of the church, notice the remnants of the round nave, only discovered in 1927. Then leave the churchyard to walk along the track leading out to a narrow road.

2. Turn left here and begin to walk downhill between the flower covered banks which line this road. On the left is the driveway leading to Church Farm and the ancient dovecote, which was built by the Knights Hospitallers and dates from 1326; it contains spaces for 666 birds. Continue down the road which soon divides and take the right fork. Pass the isolated houses of Upper Town and then Lower town on the right, and soon the wonderful views of hills all around are enhanced by the views down to the tree lined

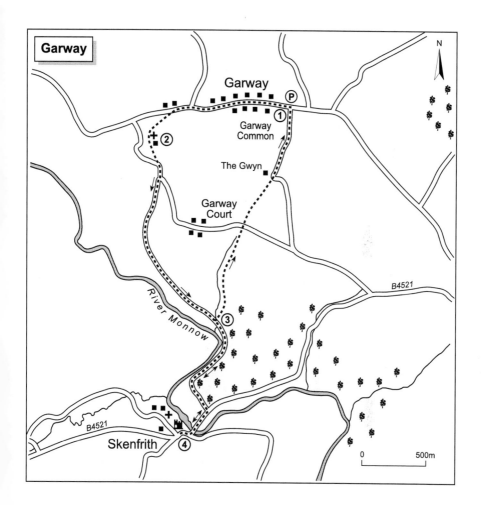

River Monnow on your right. Follow the lane for just over a mile, and when the road levels off and is beginning to bend to the right, on the left will be seen a stile. The footpath here is heading uphill alongside the fence and hedge on the left margin of the field. This is the route of your return walk to Garway.

3. But first, continue along the road as far as the major road B4521 and turn right to visit the attractive small village of Skenfrith. Cross over the Monnow bridge and on the left is the Bell Inn, formerly a 17th century coaching inn and now an award winning

Skenfrith Castle

pub and restaurant. On the right are the castle ruins and the church. The church of St Bridget dates from the 13th century, and its most striking feature from the outside is the unusual squat tower, and a large buttress because of the slightly unstable foundations. Interior features include wooden carvings, examples of 15th century embroidery and a Jacobean pew. The castle was one of three castles built by Marcher Lords to subjugate the Welsh, but unlike many castles, was built on low ground in a valley. There was certainly a castle on the site in 1160 and King Henry ordered a stone castle to be built, though he subsequently cancelled the order. But it was soon built and was in use by 1193. More stone work was added by Hubert de Burgh in 1219, rebuilt and enlarged in the 14th century, and was finally abandoned in 1538 – and then fell into ruin Although it has occasionally suffered from flooding many well preserved features have survived, including the walls and most notably the round keep. Now the ruins are well maintained by CADW.

4. After visiting Skenfrith, retrace steps to point number 3. Once over the stile stay close to the hedge and fence. There is a small valley, now often dry, parallel to the hedge. Notice a marker post on the route of the major gas pipeline which crosses the countryside here on its way from Milford Haven. Pass a small wood on the left and reach the stile at the end of a large field. Go straight ahead along the margin of the next field to reach another stile and a narrow road. Cross over here and go through a large metal gate and keep straight ahead, but with the hedge now on your right. Climb steadily to pass to the right of a large modern barn and a smart stone house, to walk along the drive and out onto the road. Keep straight ahead and this leads past a few houses and comes out on the large open space opposite the Moon.

20. Herefordshire Beacon

A circuit from Wynds Point climbs up to the British Camp, then passes Walms Well and Swinyard Hill before entering Eastnor Park to visit the memorial obelisk. The return walk is along the eastern sides of Swinyard Hill and the Herefordshire Beacon.

Distance and time	Just over 5 miles – requiring 2.5-3 hours
Terrain	Steep climb to start the walk but otherwise gentle and undulating. Only two stiles on this route. Firm paths on the hills but often muddy in News Wood
How to get there	On the A449 from Malvern to Ledbury, at the highest point on this road where it crosses the hills
Starting point	The large car park at GR 763404, on the A449 Malvern to Ledbury road
Refreshments	Snack bar and the excellent Malvern Hills Hotel at the starting point
Tourist Information Centre	Great Malvern (01684 892289)
Other places of interest	The small towns of Ledbury and Upton on Severn
Maps	OS Explorer 190 or 1:10,000 Harvey map of the Malvern Hills

The walk

1. From the top of the car park opposite the Malvern Hills hotel, and close to an information board, go through the large wooden gate along the path signed to the Herefordshire Beacon. Pass the old notice board with information about the Herefordshire Beacon or British Camp – 'Height 1115 feet (338m). One of the finest

earthworks in Britain dating from about the 2nd century BC, but later enlarged etc.'

Climb steeply through trees, and after about 40 yards turn sharp right and zig-zag, just following the surfaced path. Because it is steep you gain height quickly and soon emerge above the trees where wonderful views open up across the Severn plain to the Cotswolds. The top of the camp is also visible, as you reach the first of the embankments and ditches. Various paths and options can be seen, but just follow the surfaced path (one of very few locations in the Malvern Hills where paths have been surfaced, and an indication of the popularity of this route). Looking back to the north, there is a perfect view along the ridge; it can be seen how the line of the ridge is offset near British Camp because of ancient faulting, which moved the crustal rocks slightly to one side. It is almost certain to be windy near the summit as you move into a different meteorological zone from that experienced down near the car park. Cross the ditches and embankments and wonder about the time and energy involved in digging and moving earth to shape these features.

Looking north along the Malvern Ridge

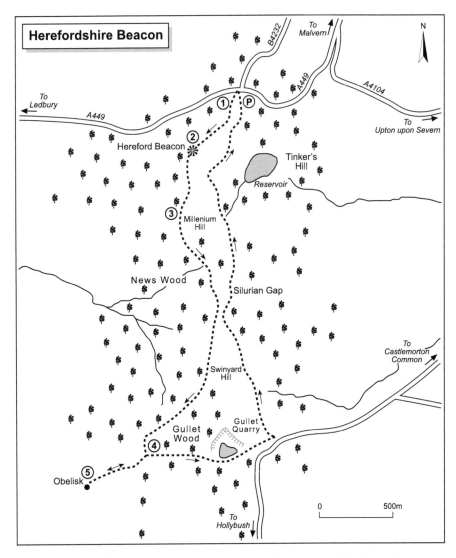

2. Once the all round views have been admired and before the wind
   blows you over, head southwards, descending slightly to the large
   flatter area where the Iron Age settlement was located. Keep near
   the right side of this flattish area and at its lowest point, before the
   slight rise towards the southern edge of the fort, look for the path
   going down to the right. This is a clear grassy path which heads

steeply down across an embankment and a ditch, towards the woods. As you descend there is a clear view of a large farm complex (Ockeridge Farm) and the main road to Ledbury beyond. To the left of this farm is another set of farm buildings (Netherton Farm), and further to the left is Eastnor Castle and then Eastnor Obelisk. Also prominent are the trees on the top of May Hill, and perhaps the Black Mountains with Hay Bluff at the northern end, and Sugar Loaf in the hills near Abergavenny. The path leads into the woods, with shelter from the weather.

3. Reach a horizontal path where you turn left and go on over the stile onto a broad track – which may have muddy patches. Patches of ramsons (wild garlic) cover the floor of the woods around here. The track begins to descend, and a few views open to the right, especially where there has been recent clearing work. And there may still be forestry work going on around here, or even Land Rovers showing their versatility on the forest tracks. Flowers will cover the forest floor in spring and early summer and, at this time of the year, many warblers and other birds will be singing. Reach a cross tracks (very steep to the left, used for Range Rover trials), but keep straight on, descending slightly. At another cross tracks steep slopes lead to right and left, but keep straight on. Bluebells are abundant in this area. Reach a gate with a stile alongside and just before this, on the left, is Walms Well, thought to have been used by Iron Age settlers about 250BC. On the right is the covered storage reservoir used to supply Eastnor Castle and village. Once over the stile keep straight ahead, ignoring the right turn to a metal gate. Climb steadily along a sunken track and soon pass a path going off to the left (this leads to Silurian Gap – to be reached later). The wood opens up a little and the track is nearly level. To the left now, is Swinyard Hill. Reach a cattle grid and gates, and keep straight ahead here. A drier path runs parallel to the main track, which is often very muddy. Follow this route winding through the woods, until reaching a major cross paths.

4. Turn left here – but first it is worthwhile to go right, through the gate into Eastnor Park. There is a choice four paths; select the second from the left, more or less straight ahead and rising slightly. From this path there are good views left up to Midsummer Hill, the location of another Iron Age fort, and looking down is the

valley where the ruins of Bronsil Hall are hidden by the trees. This old house was the home of Lord Beauchamp who was Lord Treasurer to Henry VI. The path leads to the 90ft high obelisk perched on the grassy hilltop. Erected in 1812 this is a family memorial to the Honourable Edward Charles Cocks. The inscriptions on all sides have been well worn by the weather. In this part of Eastnor Park the areas of bracken are home to the rare High Brown Fritillary butterflies which lay eggs on the violets, which flower before the bracken growth covers them. Part of Eastnor Park is used as a caravan and camping site, and is home to

The Obelisk

a fine herd of red deer, as well as being used as a testing area for Range Rovers. The castle itself overlooks the lake and deer park and was designed for the 1st Earl Somers by Sir Robert Smirke, who also designed the British Museum. It is still a family home but is also a popular location for weddings and has many tourist attractions including displays of armour and paintings and a children's play area.

5. Turn round and retrace steps to leave Eastnor Park (point 4 again) and go ahead along the broad stony track which descends through the woods. This valley is the Gullet and leads down to the fairly dramatic Gullet Lake in the old quarry – a very popular location for Geology students. This deep lake can look tempting on hot summer's day, but the water is always cold and swimming is dangerous and to be avoided. Walk alongside the lake to reach a useful information board which tells something of the geology. Once beyond the information board walk along the narrow road

passing two houses and just before reaching a major road, turn left along the stony track. This is the gradual climb up the east side of Swinyard Hill. Join this ridge where it has descended to the hollow known as Silurian Gap, so called because of a change of rock types, and an outcrop of Silurian age rocks. Several paths meet here and you keep straight ahead on the path signed to 'Giants Cave and British Camp', climbing quite steeply for a short distance. The broad and worn path soon divides, with right going to Hangmans Hill and Broad Down but keep left towards the cave. Walk on through a small wood then out into open grassland. Pass the cave where a hermit once lived, and climb slightly to another marker stone and follow the arrow to British Camp hotel and Wynds point. The southern gate of the camp is up to your left, with a stone-paved path to protect the hill from too much erosion. The fairly level broad track moves along the side of the hill, with the fort up to your left and the reservoir down to the right. This slope is where wheatears and redstarts may be seen in spring and summer. Walk across this open hillside with good views down to Little Malvern and across the Severn plain. Re-enter the woods, and follow the broad path descending steadily to the car park and hotel.

The lake in Gullet Quarry

21. Worcester

The walk is alongside the river and on the canal towpath, with short stretches along the pavements, exploring some of Worcester's fascinating history, as well as modern day attractions. Easy walking on flat and dry terrain, and there are no stiles.

Distance and time	5 miles – 2-3 hours
Terrain	Mostly level and along firm clear paths and roads
How to get there	In the centre of Worcester there are car parks close to the river and the racecourse (best avoided on race days)
Starting point	At the Severn Bridge in Worcester, within sight of the cathedral. GR 846548
Refreshments	A good choice in Worcester
Tourist Information Centre	Worcester (phone 01905 726311)
Other places of interest	Malvern Hills nearby and many historical features in Worcester
Maps	OS Explorer 204; Landranger 150

The walk

1. Start from the main bridge and walk upstream on the town side of the river, passing the Old Rectifying House and Severn View Hotel. A plaque on the wall to the left shows a railway engine and gives the information about The Butts Spur line, built about 1860 to link Foregate Street station to the river. Stay on the river side and look for the plaque on your right, explaining this is the Le Vesinet Promenade and that Worcester's medieval bridge crossed the

Severn here. Bridge Gate was on a pier in the middle, until it was demolished in 1702. The riverside is colourful with hanging baskets in summer and is lined by many trees. Walk on, beyond where Pride of the Midlands sails from, on short cruises for tourists, and then pass beneath the magnificent viaduct carrying the Worcester to Hereford railway line. Built to enable the railway to travel from Foregate Street station without having to descend to river level, it dates from 1860 but was rebuilt with iron girders in 1904 – and has recently been cleaned and restored. A few yards further along is the Footbridge and Cycle Way, dating from 1992 and named after Sabrina, the river Goddess of the Severn. Pass the Rowing Club and then either behind the Stand close to the river, or in front of the Grandstand, to continue along the path lined by an avenue of lime trees to head north along the edge of Pitchcroft.

2. At the north end of the race-course you reach the Boat House, and go through the iron gate and along the road, as it bends round to

The recent footbridge over the River Severn

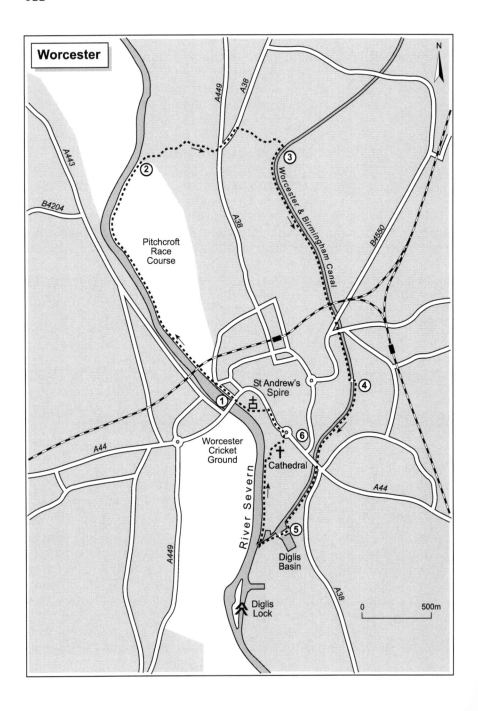

the Environment Centre. This is located in the old Pump House of the Severn Trent Waterworks, Barbourne (Open Wednesdays to Saturday 10 am until 4pm – free entry. Light refreshments served. Phone 01905 23267). You are on Waterworks Road, and where Pope Iron road goes right, turn left following the footpath sign 'Riverside and Northwick'. Cross the open grassy area, with the river away to the left and Gheluvelt Park to the right.

The park opened on 17th June, 1922 to commemorate the Worcestershire Regiment 2nd Battalion's part in the Battle of Gheluvelt near Ypres on 31st October, 1914. Beyond Barbourne Brook reach a road where you turn right. Walk along Lavender Road, with houses on the left and the park on the right. Reach the main road at the junction of Ombersley Road and the Droitwich Road and cross over both of them, passing the Old Toll House, then turn left up the Droitwich Road. A short distance up the slope take the first right turning, Gregory's Mill Street. Keep straight ahead along here, between houses and light industries, and when the road bends to the left, look for Canal Side where you turn right. Pass many modern houses to the left to reach the canal and, with bridge 13 and a lock on your left, turn right.

3. Walk along the towpath, also used by Monarch's Way long distance footpath. Soon pass the Worcester City football ground at St Georges Lane on the right. To the left opposite here is a housing development on the site of the old Brick Works, where a small BBC station was located during World War II and was prepared for use in emergencies. If the government had been driven from London by German invasion or bombing it might have moved to Hindlip Hall near Worcester, and here, in the brickyard was a small radio station from where the government would broadcast to the country. The Cavalier pub is on the right, and you pass beneath bridge 12, following the dry and firm path alongside the canal – accompanied by swans, ducks and moorhens. Pass Flagge Meadow on the right, the playing fields of Worcester Royal Grammar School, and continue beneath the next bridge with a children's playground area and another sports field of the Worcester RGS to your right. Allotments, across the canal, slope up towards the Rainbow Hill district of Worcester, and modern houses line the bank on the right. As we approach the centre of the city, pass

beneath the railway line and on your right is the Sorting Office and then the Lowesmoor Boatyard.

4. There are traffic noises and signs of old industrial development along the next stretch, and then the clock tower of Heenan and Froude engineering company is on the left – now the Shrub Hill Industrial site. When Pizza Hut is on the left go up on to the road and cross over to the other side of the canal, but just continue along the towpath, passing more modern housing developments on both sides. A stretch of reeds on the opposite side of the canal attracts birds and provides a suitable site for swans to nest. Pass Blockhouse lock and cottage, and soon reach the Fownes Hotel, a former glove making factory, on your right. On the left is the Commandery, now a very informative museum, which has a remarkable history from Civil War times. The Commandery was founded by St Wulstan the Bishop of Worcester in about 1085 and used as a hospital and almshouses. It was used as an escape route by King Charles II, and is the starting point of Monarch's Way, which traces the route taken by Charles II as he made his escape to France.

    Pass Sidbury Lock and keep straight ahead to the Diglis Basin. The towpath is also a cycle route – number 45. The site of the Royal Worcester Porcelain factory (now sadly closed) is across to our right as we reach the Diglis moorings. Turn left at the large basin, crowded with boats. Pass the Anchor on the left and then the Grist Mill Boatyard sign on your right. On the left is the main entrance into Diglis Basin Marina, but turn right here – with boats moored on the left, and the basin is surrounded by smart modern developments. Walk over a wooden swing bridge and, after about 20 yards, turn right over another wooden swing bridge. Turn left at the British Waterways Information Office to pass the clear map on the wall, with Diglis Top Lock on the right. Walk on to the Bottom Lock and the banks of the Severn and the end (or beginning) of the Worcester-Birmingham canal.

5. Just to the left here is the main Diglis Lock on the River Severn, but you turn right, over the swinging footbridge to walk upstream. Pass the newish finger post pointing to 'Birmingham (30 miles and 58 locks), and Stourport (14 miles with 3 locks)'. Walk along the

Worcester cathedral viewed from the road bridge

bankside footpath and the cathedral tower comes into view, but even more prominent is the graceful spire of St Andrews. Birds and boats are likely to be seen on the tree lined river as you walk past the Sea Scouts base, then a row of neat terraced houses. The very smart Diglis Hotel is on the right and the Diglis Parade changes to Kleve Walk as you continue upstream, passing the Kings School Boathouse and the site of a summer ferry. Turn right at the Water Gate, where the highest flood levels have been marked, and there is a plaque to tell you that a ferry has operated at this site for many centuries – with a break between the 1950s and 1983. Go through the gate and up the steps onto the College Green, surrounded by buildings which are now part of the Kings School. The entrance to the cathedral is on the left, and either walk through here or proceed to the Great Gate in Edgar Tower archway at the far end of the Green and turn left to follow the road round to the far side of the cathedral.

The cathedral is magnificent and well worth a visit. Dating from the 7th century, it was rebuilt later and the present building was begun in 1084. Changes and repairs continued through the centuries and much of the exterior dates from Victorian times. Amongst the many highlights to be seen inside are the tomb of King John in the chancel, close to the main altar, and the tomb of Arthur Prince of Wales, the elder brother of King Henry VIII. Amongst other interesting features are the remarkable east and west windows and memorials to Edward Elgar and members of the Beauchamp family.

6. Leave the cathedral by the main door and walk out to the main road and the war memorial for the Boer War. Turn left down Deansway passing the Old Palace then the small St Alban's church, which may have originated in Roman times but certainly there was a church here in 720AD. The present building is early Norman from about 1175. Try to ignore the less attractive buildings of the Technical College. At the traffic lights turn left down Copenhagen Street, with the tower and spire of the Glover's Needle (St Andrews) on the right. In recent years a peregrine falcon has nested on the platform at the base of the spire, which reaches up to a height of 155 ft. Four young were successfully reared in 2009. The cathedral and St Andrew's spire sit at the top of the valley side and your route descends to the fountain and turn right along the river bank. The County Cricket Ground is across the river to the left. Just before reaching the bridge notice the plaque in the wall on the left of the footpath, telling you that John Gwynn (sometimes spelt with an e) was the architect of the bridge built in the 1770s to replace a stone bridge, built by monks in 1313. Another plaque commemorates the widening of the present bridge in 1931.

22. Upper Arley to Trimpley

This scenic walk takes you downstream alongside the Severn, then passes the reservoirs before climbing through the woods, crossing farmland on the return towards Arley. The whistle of the Severn Valley Railway trains is likely to be heard at some point of the walk in the summer months, and a ride on the train or a visit to the Arboretum are added attractions to a visit to Upper Arley.

Distance and time	4 miles for the circuit, plus additional short walks up to the church and across the river to Arley station. 2-3 hours – or longer if visiting the Arboretum
Terrain	Gentle alongside the river then a steady climb into the woods followed by the descent back to the village
How to get there	From the A442 Kidderminster to Bridgnorth road, turn left at Shatterford, signed to Upper Arley, and turn right just before reaching the river
Starting point	Car park and picnic area near the River Severn in Upper Arley. Pay and Display (£1 for the day). GR 764802
Refreshments	Café in the village, small café in Arley Arboretum, pub across the footbridge, and pub at the main road in Shatterford
Tourist Information Centre	Bewdley (phone 01299 404740)
Other places of interest	Hampton Loade with its unusual ferry, Dudmaston Hall (NT) and Bridgnorth
Maps	OS Landranger 138; Explorer 218

Upper Arley was an agricultural village which grew near the river and spread up the valley side, with the church perched on the top. Adjacent to the church was Arley Castle, built in 1844 by Earl Mountnorris, who also designed the Arboretum. The castle was demolished in the 1970s and has been replaced by a modern house. The river crossing was a chain ferry, until replaced by the footbridge in 1964.

The Arboretum is one of the oldest in Britain and contains more than 300 species of trees. First planted in 1820 by Lord Mountnorris and taken over by Robert Woodward and family in 1852. Though particularly colourful in autumn, with acers, maples, and a large display of fungi, it is lovely throughout the year, with spring flowers and azaleas early in the year. The selection of conifers includes some giants, notably Cedar of Lebanon and Wellingtonia, and the Crimean pines with almost vertical branches – and there are grand deciduous trees too. Mr Roger Turner, a Staffordshire Industrialist and philanthropist bought the estate in 1959, and restored the Arboretum

Arboretum gardens

and the walled gardens. He also restored many buildings and constructed new houses in the village. He died in 1999 but left the estate to the Charitable Trust he had founded. It is now open to the public from March to November, on Wednesdays to Sundays and Bank Holiday Mondays 11am to 5 pm. The charge for admission is £5. Phone number 01299 861368. (www.arley-arboretum.org.uk)

The Severn Valley Railway links Kidderminster with Bridgnorth, and from Bewdley to Bridgnorth closely follows the River Severn. Trains run every weekend throughout the year and daily from May to the beginning of October. In October the service operates at weekends and daily through the school half term week (Phone 01299 403816 or www.svr.co.uk).

The Walk

1. Walk from the car park heading downstream, passing a small toilet block. Turn left to walk up the hill to visit the church. Pass the fine Glebe House and turreted building on the left, and the Old Post Office opposite, with a clock on its wall. Beyond a short row of houses you reach the church. Just before entering the churchyard, notice a path through the gate to the right. If wishing to visit the Arboretum this is one possible route to take, but also, there is a small gate leading from the left side of the church. Close to this gate is the very modest grave of Mr Roger Turner (1923-99). Described as 'Man of Industry, the church and this village'.

The sandstone church of St Peter dates mostly from the 14th century, though small fragments of the older Norman building can be seen on the south wall of the nave. Good use has been made of local materials, as the church is built of local stone from Hexton's Quarry near Arley, and oak trees from the Arley Estate provided the wood for pews and the altar. There was much rebuilding in 1885 and a fine Kempe window at the east end is from 1887. Various family memorials to the owners of the estate Sir Henry Lyttleton and Viscount Valentia are prominent on the south wall. Note the 14th century effigy in the north chapel – probably the knight Walter de Balun who was the first husband of Isolda Mortimer. He died in a tournament on his wedding day – in 1270.

Walk back downhill from the church, passing the turning to the car park and then the location of the old ferry on the right – where ducks may be waiting to be fed. Then reach the Riverside Tea Rooms, with a terrace opposite overlooking the river – and next is the Post Office. The road bends left out of the village and you fork right to the footbridge.

Two reasons for crossing the footbridge – either now or at the end of the walk – are the 16th century Harbour Inn and the very picturesque Severn Valley Railway station. From the footbridge enjoy the excellent views up and downstream, with ducks and swans on the water, gulls flying around and, in summer, sand martins will be chasing insects low over the water. These summer visitors from Africa nest in holes in the sandy banks of the river.

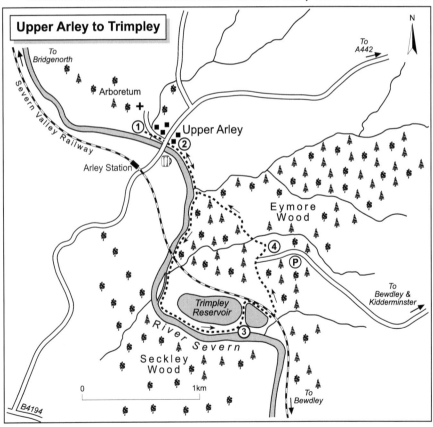

View to Upper Arley from the station

2. Walking downstream on the left side of the river, follow the riverside path signed 'North Worcestershire Way and the Severn Way' with its logo of the Trow. These old sailing vessels used to travel up and down the Severn from Bristol to Bridgnorth and Ironbridge. In the 17th and 18th centuries the Severn was the equivalent of the present day M6. Pass a few buildings to the left and just beyond the small stream, where the path divides, keep right along the river bank. Cross a small stile as you pass beneath the imposing Victoria Bridge, built at Coalbrookdale in 1861. Reach another stile and emerge into an open field and an information board welcoming us to Trimpley Reservoirs, which provide additional water supplies for Birmingham and have been pumping water from the river since 1967.

3. Move away from the river and climb the grassy slope to the top of the embankment. Fork right along this embankment to walk round the reservoir. A popular fishing and sailing location this is also the home to many ducks, swans, great crested grebes and gulls. In the summer, terns, swallows and house martins may be seen flying

over the water. Grey wagtails search for food along the lake margin. Leave the embankment via the wooden steps to the narrow road between the two reservoirs, and follow the sign to Eymore Wood car park. Turn left to move away from the reservoir and cross the railway line. Go through the small gate into the wood. The path immediately divides and you go straight ahead and begin to climb. Follow this broad and stony or cobbled path, and bend left where it is joined by a path from the right. Fork left when the path divides, cross an open strip and climb slightly to reach a narrow road. The entrance to Severn Trent buildings is on the left. Cross this road, noting that the Eymore Wood car park and picnic site is a few yards to the right (and could be used as an alternative starting point if desired).

4. Walk on through the gate, and the track leads through woods to a major cross tracks. Turn left here, following the sign for the 'North Worcestershire Way' with its logo of the fir cone. The stony drive leads to Huntsfield Cottage, and just before reaching the gate across this drive, move right, over a stile into a field, and follow the left margin of this field. Pass the house on the left and go on through the kissing gate and cross an open field, whilst enjoying the views ahead, over the Severn into Shropshire. Descend slightly to another kissing gate, then cross another grassy field with isolated hawthorns, possibly laden with berries, to reach a stile and the edge of the woods. Once over the stile descend quite steeply to the riverside path. Turn right here to reach the footbridge and point number 2.

23. Kingsford Country Park

Walk in the Country Park and along Kinver Edge, through delightful mixed woodland and heath rich in wild life. Views across the surrounding countryside are outstanding especially in winter when the trees are bare. Springtime flowers, bird song and autumnal colours are other seasonal attractions.,

Distance and time	6 miles, with a short cut option of 4 miles if required. Time required 2-3 hours
Terrain	Clear paths through the woods. Mostly fairly level or gently undulating, but with one short climb. The ground can become muddy in the woods, although the sandy paths dry quickly, and the paths are very firm along Kinver Edge. No stiles on this walk
How to get there	Take the A442 north from Kidderminster for one mile, then turn right along the B4190 to Wolverley. Turn right on the B4189 signed towards Stourbridge, and soon take the first left. Follow the brown and white signs to Kingsford Country Park from Wolverley village, and drive along Blakeshall Lane
Starting point	GR 834821
Refreshments	Choice of pubs in Wolverley and even more choice in Kinver
Tourist Information Centre	Kidderminster – phone 01299 404740
Other places of interest	Kinver village and caves in the sandstone; Safari Park
Maps	OS Explorer 218 or 219; Landranger 138

Kingsford Forest Park covers 200 acres of pine-birch woodland with areas of open heath. Adjacent to Kinver Edge, which extends northwards from the Park. Areas of commercial forest with pine and larch were developed between 1930-1960. The Park is a sandstone area, but in places is quite soft and has been excavated. Families created dwellings in the sandstone – especially in the 18th century when the Hyde iron works in

Old caves, no longer inhabited

Kinver opened, and workers arrived in the area. Most are now derelict and out of bounds, but near to Kinver, Holy Austin rock house, owned by the National Trust, is open for visitors. The Rock Houses had been in use since the 1600s, and the last tenants abandoned the cave houses in 1964.

The walk

1. Start from Kingsford Country Park parking and picnic site on Blakeshall Lane. By the information board is a finger post and you follow the sign pointing to 'North Worcestershire Path, Wythall'. The North Worcestershire Path leads through the trees, away from the car park, and roughly parallel to the road you arrived on. Reach the road near Oakleigh and walk along the road between very smart houses. Pass a path to the left and you are then joined by a path from the right. Keep going along Blakeshall Lane and pass several houses of Blakeshall, then fork off to the right along a bridle path between a private drive to the right and houses to the left. This leads through to another narrow road where you turn right.

2. After about 50 yards, as the road bends left, go ahead with a sandstone wall to your right and take the sandy track which begins to descend. Blakeshall House is to the right. The sandy track bends to the left and you pass the 'Welcome to Kingsford Forest Park' notice. As the path levels off, a cross paths is reached, with fences

to prevent horses moving left or right. Turn right here, along the North Worcestershire Path, still following the fir cone logo. At the next junction of paths do not turn sharp right, but go ahead a few yards and then right along the main track, which is continues up the hill. Here, as in many parts of this walk, there are likely to be an abundance of birds noises – woodpeckers, nuthatch, jay, various tits – and the omnipresent robin. At a fairly level and slightly open patch, where the main track goes straight on, turn right on a broad grassy track following the fir cone, the woodpecker trail and coal tit trail. Climb up the hill passing many

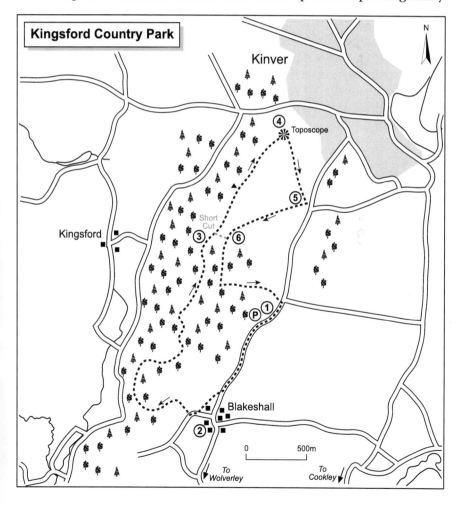

sweet chestnut trees and at the top of the hill reach a major junction of paths. Turn left here still following the fir cone, to walk up to the Severn Trent Blakeshall covered reservoir, where you turn right and then left to continue along the North Worcestershire Path. The views really open up now, as you look out west towards Castle Hill and the Severn Valley. The path stays close to the steep edge, with views through the trees. Reach a large turning to the right, which leads back to the car park – but continue straight ahead. The footpath sign has North Worcestershire Path, Woodpecker Trail and Nuthatch Trail pointing back the way we have come and the Staffordshire Way pointing ahead. Continuing northwards the path soon divides but just keep left and stay close to the edge. As you proceed, reach the 'NT Kinver Edge' sign, beyond which the path divides. Left fork continues on the edge of the steep slope, but the right fork moves to the east following the boundary of the National Trust land.

3. For the short cut route, turn right here, close to the fence and walk on as far as a gate and an open field (point 6). Turn right here, before the gate, and stay close to the fence on your left as you walk downhill through the woods to reach a broad track where you turn left. Pass the Kinver Edge Farm on the left and return to the car park starting point.

For the longer option keep straight ahead along the top of the Edge – and enjoy the views. Reach the triangulation point at 164m. All round views reveal Clee Hill to the west; Dudley and Stourbridge ahead and tower blocks on the edge of the West Midlands conurbation; Clent Hills and the Wychbury Obelisk stand up away to your right. You are following the red trail now. Paths go to right and left near an old brick building but just keep

Views towards Kinver

ahead. The long flat area, as you approach the toposcope, is the site of an old Iron Age fort, and an open area used for grazing.

4. Turn right from the toposcope, with two main paths to chose from. The left fork has a blue marker but take the right fork, with the red marker – and go slightly downhill on the broad stony track with pebbles from the Bunter sandstones. As you approach the open grassy area, on the left is a plaque set in a large rock, which commemorates the meeting on 29th September, 1917 when 200 acres were given to the National Trust. A little further on the left is the granite war memorial followed by the information board and map, just a few yards before reaching the narrow road and a popular parking area. Do not go as far as the road, but instead turn sharp right at the information board to walk along the left margin of the open grassy area.

    The information board says that Kinver Edge is a sandstone ridge with unusual rock houses (caves – but enlarged by digging out) panoramic views, heather and woodland. The National Trust has responsibility to manage the 128 hectares (318 acres) with woods, heathland, Iron Age fort and caves.

5. From the information board follow the broad clear path. Soon reach the open grassy patch with signs of recent felling – this is part of the management process to remove woodland and enable heathland to extend over a larger area – as it used to in the past. Move slightly left to a wooden kissing gate and keep ahead with wire fencing and an open field to the left. Near this sandy path are acorns and fungi in the autumn and gorse bushes in flower at most seasons.

6. Once through the next wooden kissing gate turn left to go downhill in a coniferous area, with a wire fence on the left – as mentioned earlier for the short cut option. This leads down to a major track where you turn left along the broad track by a wooden fence. Pass the entrance to Kinver Edge Farm and soon arrive back at the starting point.

24. Lickey Hills and Bittell Reservoirs

Hills, woods, fields and lakes are all part of this walk, as we explore an area of ancient rocks which have created a playground area for Birmingham.

Distance and time	4½ miles requiring 2 hours
Terrain	A slope down through woods in the first part of the walk and a climb back up to the finish, with only gentle undulations to pass Barnt Green and the Bittell Reservoirs
How to get there	Travel north from Bromsgrove along the B4096 to the Lickeys and turn right when signed to Lickey Hills Country Park Visitor Centre
Starting point	Lickey Hills Visitor Centre GR 998754
Refreshments	At the Visitor Centre or pubs nearby in Rednal and Barnt Green
Tourist Information Centre	Bromsgrove 01527 831809
Other places of interest	Clent Hills, Hagley Park and Hall, Jewellery Quarter in Birmingham
Maps	OS Explorer 220; Landranger139

Lickey Hills consist of old hard rocks, including 600 million year old quartzite, some of the oldest rocks in England. These rocks are so hard that they still form high ground and have helped to create a playground area for the inhabitants of Birmingham just to the north. Visitors can enjoy the attractive rural landscapes so close to Birmingham. The Lickey Country Park was designated in 1971 and covers an area of 212 hectares (over 520 acres). The Visitor Centre opened in 1990 (phone 01214477106) and is an information centre as well as offering refreshments. The Lickey landscape consists of areas of deciduous woodland, stands of coniferous trees, scrubby heathland and grassy areas as well as areas of bilberry. The varied vegetation attracts a wide range of birds including crossbills and siskins in winter.

The walk

1. Walk past the Visitor Centre, heading downhill. Pass to the left of the Children's Playground and then the Arboretum, with over 70 varieties of tree, and the wooden carved statue of *The Spirit of the Woods* by Graham Jones. Continue along the broad path, downhill through the woods. When the path divides take the right fork signed to Barnt Green and continue downhill. At a junction of paths turn right, over a stream and begin to climb. This broad and stony cobbled path (possibly from Bunter pebble beds) through the oak and beech trees bends to the left and passes occasional

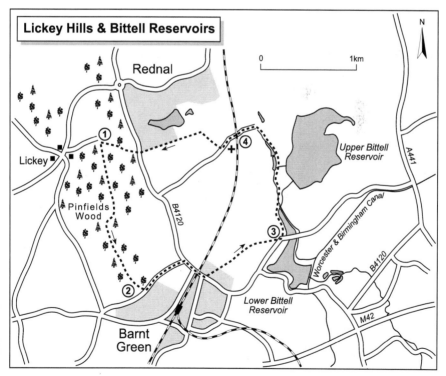

seats. Continue through the attractive ancient Pinfields Wood, full of bluebells and other wild flowers in spring. Reach a gate and a narrow road where you turn left for 10 yards and then right along the broad footpath into a small wood. Keep ahead along an avenue of trees between gardens to reach Barnt Green, opposite the station.

Spirit of the woods carved statue

2. Turn left along this road and at the T-junction reach a major road, the B4120, and turn right along Bittell Road to pass beneath the railway bridge. Follow the road signed to Alvechurch for about 50 yards and then turn left alongside the Baptist church, to walk through to the Playing Fields. Head for the far left corner of the field, go through a small wood and over the stile by a stream, then along the left margin of the field. At the end of this field head diagonally right across the middle of the next field, passing to the right of the small pond. At the end of this field go through the small wooden gate and turn left along the stony track signed 'Private Road – Authorised Vehicles only'. Before walking along here stroll a few yards along the road straight ahead to look into the Lower Bittell Reservoir, on the right, and the overflow pool, to the left. Both are popular with birds, ducks, swans, geese and gulls – and with fishermen too. The reservoir was created to maintain the flow of water to the mills on the River Arrow.

3. Follow the broad track between hedges, with fields on the left and the wetland of Mill Shrub to the right. Climb slightly and soon

notice a small stream on the left and the sluice gate which enables the water to pass beneath the track. At a small pond the track bends right and then left and you keep ahead alongside what becomes a surfaced narrow road, to pass the two ponds. But first, make a detour through the gate to the right along the grassy track to have a look at the Upper Bittell reservoir. Pass the old buildings of the Pump House which contained a steam engine made by Boulton, Watt and Co, and used for pumping water up into the reservoir. The reservoir dates from 1790s, when it was built as a feeder for the Worcester-Birmingham canal. It is a very popular lake for boating and fishing but also for ornithologists who may see a variety of ducks including sawbills, as well as geese, grebes and gulls, with herons and cormorants often see around the edges. Climb up the embankment around the edge of the reservoir, to look at the birds and also for the boats used by members of Barnt Green Boat Club. Move back to the narrow road and walk on, to pass the entrance to Barnt Green Fishing Club and Boating Club, and then the castellated Tower House. Bend left, just following the road.

4. Pass beneath the busy railway line and detour through the churchyard to see the church of St Michael and All Angels at Cofton Hackett. This has been the site of a church for many centuries but the present building is mainly from 1861, although the timber porch is 16th century. In the church-yard, close to the porch, is the remnant of an old church cross. About 100 yards further along the road look for the metal gate and footpath to the right, signed 'North Worcestershire Path'. Follow this alongside the margin of the field and then bend left across the higher part of the field to reach a metal gate. Keep straight ahead across the

Stone head on Cofton Hackett church

path to a second gate, then walk along the margin of the next field, to another gate. Keep straight ahead, now with houses and gardens to the right, and reach a wooden kissing gate and a narrow footpath between houses and gardens, to reach the road B4120. Cross the road and climb steeply up through the woods, helped by the wooden steps. Reach a cross paths and turn right here following the fir cone logo. Continue climbing and this leads back to the car park at the Visitor Centre.

To enjoy the wonderful views over Birmingham, before going into the car park and the Visitor Centre, veer slightly to the right to the top of the car parks and the edge of the hill. From here can be seen much of Birmingham including the former site of the motor car factory just down at the bottom of the hill in Longbridge, and the lights of football grounds and Birmingham airport can be seen in the distance. Along the edge of the hill (which is named Bilberry Hill - for obvious reasons) you may notice old dew ponds which date from the time this land was used for pasture by the Earls of Plymouth, who owned this area from the 16th century.

25. Stourport and Hartlebury Common

Beginning and ending on different sections of Hartlebury Common, the walk also takes us along an old railway line, on the canal towpath and through the Canal Basin in Stourport, as well as a short stretch alongside the Severn. This walk will appeal to anyone interested in boats, old forms of transport or the natural history of the Common.,

Distance and time	5½ miles requiring between 2 and 3 hours
Terrain	Two short hills in the early part of the walk but otherwise mostly level. No stiles
How to get there	Along the A4025 from Worcester to Stourport, to reach the edge of the Common near Stourport
Starting point	GR 820705 the South Car park on Hartlebury Common
Refreshments	Cafés and pubs in Stourport and the Rose and Crown along the edge of the Common, very close to the starting point (phone 01299 822676)
Tourist Information Centre	Kidderminster phone 01299 404740
Other places of interest	The riverside town of Bewdley and the Wyre Forest
Maps	OS Explorer 218; Landranger138

Stourport owes its origins to the canal – the Staffordshire and Worcestershire canal built by Brindley and opened in 1771. It gave rise to the town of Stourport, and remained very important until the 1830s, but by then the Worcester-Birmingham canal had been opened in 1815. The railways had also appeared, which contributed to the decline of Stourport.

Hartlebury Common is a remnant of a larger lowland heath – very rare nowadays in Britain, and containing a mixed vegetation cover, with gorse, heather, grasses other small plants and scattered trees. The common extends over 36 hectares (88 acres) and is owned and managed by the Worcestershire County Council Countryside Service. The Geology is mainly Bunter sands and some Keuper, of New Red Sandstone age, but with some glacial deposits on top deposited by melt water, as well as areas of windblown sands. Although mainly semi arid heathland there are a few boggy areas in lowest parts giving added variations in habitat – very good for wild life, with food and shelter for a range of insects and birds.

The walk

1. The information board in the car park bids a welcome to Hartlebury Common and the Leapgate Old Railway Line. From the car park walk at right angles to the road and head towards the top of the slope and the group of tall trees. Cross through sandy and grassy patches as well as gorse, and climb steadily up to the top of the hill. Beware of rabbit holes! Turn left to walk along the fairly level summit of the ridge, passing through gorse and more open patches as well as a good stand of coniferous trees. Look back and out to the left over Stourport to enjoy the views across to Abberley and Clee Hills. Reach the large Wilden Top car park, with its useful information board, and turn sharp right here to pass the triangulation point at the height of 56m. Follow the grassy track between fence and hedge to emerge on a broad path descending to the stables. Pass the Livery Yard and keep straight ahead, across the drive, and then along a path steeply down and then up the other side of the small valley. Follow a wooden fence on your left and walk on across a level field to pass to the right of a large house. Turn left along the driveway to pass Charlton House and reach the B4193.

2. Turn left for 20 yards and then right at Charlton Lane, and immediately on the left is the footpath sign to Leapgate. Take the broad footpath between hedges to the left of Charlton Lane, and this soon leads through to open fields with good all round views. Note Hartlebury away to the right and the twin peaks of Clent Hills a long way ahead to the right. The path heads straight across the

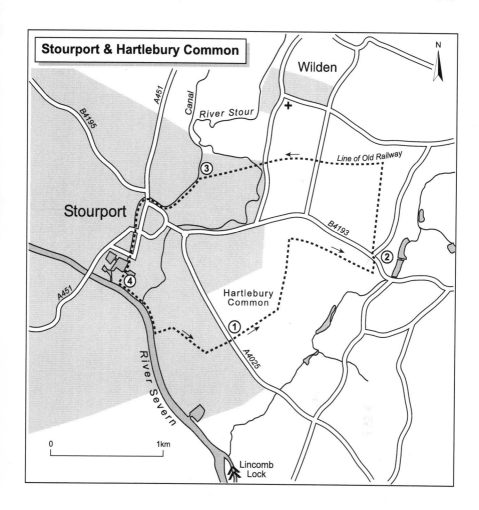

fields until the old railway line is reached, where you turn left. This is Leapgate Old Railway Line and is a designated Country Park. This leads back towards Stourport. Stay on this track for just over a mile, in a deep cutting at first, lined with trees and shrubs, with wild flowers, insects and birds – and several outcrops of red sandstone. Pass beneath a bridge carrying a narrow road and then high over another road. A few yards down to the left is the Rock Tavern, and about 200 yards to the right along this road is All Saints Church in Wilden – noted for its Burne-Jones windows. The church was built at the expense of the Baldwin family whose money had come from their iron works. Sir Edward Burne-Jones was the brother-in-law of Alfred Baldwin, whose son Stanley became Prime Minister. Cross over the River Stour, which flows from Kidderminster and joins the Severn in Stourport. An area of recent housing is to the left and there are open field to the right. When the path divides, fork right to go down to the canal where you turn left.

3. Walk alongside the canal and soon pass, or call in at, the Bird in Hand. This pub dates from 1772, but has been extended and changed since that time. The former stables for the horses which pulled the barges are now the bar. Across the canal, notice flowers and graves and on your left pass a row of old cottages. Reach Bridge No 7 with the main road just a few yards to your left. At Mitton Chapel footbridge a detour to the church of St Michael is possible if desired, but the route is really straight ahead along the canal bank. The church was designed by Sir Gilbert Scott though

Approaching Stourport

not started until after his death. It replaced the earlier church of 1791, and the small modern church is located on the site of the old Victorian Gothic church, a few remnants of which have been preserved. Continue along the canal passing Gilgal Bridge No 6 and then Baldwin's 5A just a footbridge, and Lower Mitton No 5 bridge. Reach the Lock keepers cottage dating from 1853, and the Goodnight Sweetheart Traditional Tea Room and museum. Notice the lock gate with the bent elbow shape because of the lack of space. Keep straight ahead and cross the road at Wallfield No 4 Bridge.

Walk along the left side of the Canal Basin, with the old houses labelled Ancient Monument of Special Historic Interest on your left, and the main basin to your right. Much of this has been recently renovated and there is still much development taking place to the left of the narrow road you are following. Cross over the bridge and turn right with the basin and long boats to your right and the Tontine hotel and shop on the left. The tower with the clock can be seen straight ahead and you turn left past the information board to walk alongside the locks linking the basin to the river on the right, with the Tontine Modern Flat Development to the left. Across to the right is the Funfare and the main road bridge as you come down to the Severn where you turn left.

The canal is 30 ft above the level of the Severn and is linked by two sets of locks, one broad and one narrow. The basin is surrounded by Georgian buildings, relics of the canal boom, and recently renovated as part of a major redevelopment plan.

4. Turn left to walk downstream and pass the front of The Angel, and the factory which was formerly a Vinegar Factory. Cross over the River Stour close to the breakwater and old warning sign about the cross current. There used to be a power station here, opened by Earl Baldwin in 1927 – but it closed in 1984 and was then demolished.

Stay close to the river bank with the open field to your left and houses at the top of the slope. This field was the site of the former power station. Continue along the river bank, and at the first house turn left along the footpath signed GeoPark Way. Soon reach a road where you turn right for 30 yards and then fork left, to continue along the track. Pass the barrier and keep straight ahead along the track, which runs parallel with the overhead power lines, a few yards to your left. The track leads us along the edge of the common, with houses and gardens a few yards to the right. Reach another barrier, with houses close on your right. At the end of the track bend left across the common, through an area of silver birch, and still following the line of the overhead power lines. Keep going until reaching the main road A4025, very close to the starting point.

Canal basin in Stourport

26. Chaddesley Corbett and Chaddesley Woods

Enjoy a circular walk from the delightful old village across glorious countryside and through the large nature reserve of Chaddesley Woods.

Distance and time	5 miles – time required 2-3 hours
Terrain	Gentle undulation across the countryside and in the woods. Some of the paths may be muddy after wet weather
How to get there	Along the A448 from Bromsgrove towards Kidderminster and turn right into the village. Park along the village street, or at the Talbot Inn (with permission – phone 01562 777388)
Starting point	Chaddesley Corbett village. GR 893736
Refreshments	Two excellent pubs in the village and a tea shop
Tourist Information Centres	Kidderminster (01299 404740) and Bromsgrove (01527 831809)
Other places of interest	Harvington Hall; Clent Hills
Maps	OS Landranger 139; Explorer 219

The village was named Chaddesley in Saxon times, after a local family, and the second part was added when the wealthy Corbett family arrived in Norman times. The unusual village name was featured as one of the characters in Nancy Mitford's *Love in a Cold Climate*. The interesting and attractive main street is lined with black and white buildings including two pubs. The Talbot dates from the 16th century and has a large car park, garden and children's play area. The village still contains a tea shop, post office and village school. The sandstone church of St Cassian is named after a 4th century bishop, and dates from the 12th century. Fragments from Norman times include Norman arcades in the nave, and the ancient font.

Chaddesley Woods, managed for English Nature by the Worcestershire Wildlife Trust, is a nature reserve and part has been designated an SSSI. Predominantly an oak wood it contains a variety of trees including hazel, with alder along the streams – and areas of conifers. It extends over 101 hectares, but is part of the very ancient and much larger royal hunting forest of Feckenham. As

Ancient font in the church

a mixed woodland it supports a range of wild life, and is particularly noted for the spring flowers especially bluebells, which thrive in the areas of acid soils. Other flowers, butterflies and birds are also numerous.

The walk

1. Start near the church and walk through part of the village, passing the tea room on the right. When opposite the Swan Inn turn right and pass a flower shop and the old 16th century Malt House with its stable doors. Keep straight ahead out into the fields. Reach a narrow road and continue ahead, passing the modernised Vicarage Farm on the left and follow the track. At the end of the hedge one path keeps straight ahead, but turn right alongside the hedge. The track takes you between hedge and fence, and when these end, turn left close to the fence, and then right and left again to reach a narrow path. There is a newish pond a few yards to the right, but

on the left is a well established pond, with a small island in the middle. After passing through a modern metal gate, climb to the top of the small hill – from where there are impressive views all round – back towards the Abberley and Malvern Hills, or left to the Clents. Cross the farm drive, which leads to Chaddesley Wood Farm. Go straight ahead across the middle of a large field, descending to a metal gate and a narrow path between fences to reach the edge of the woods – and another metal gate. The path goes alongside the edge of the woods to a driveway. Turn left here and walk to the gate at the entrance of the woods, and a notice welcoming you to the National Nature Reserve of Chaddesley Woods.

2. Continue straight ahead and climb steadily along the track, to reach an information board where a track joins from the left. Parts of the wood have been planted with conifers since 1935 but there have been recent plans to thin them out, and open up wider areas

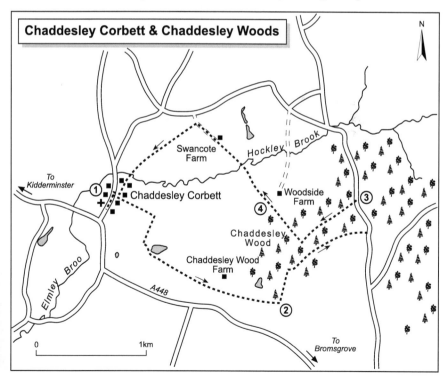

Chaddesley Corbett & Chaddesley Woods

and lighter glades. As you walk through the woods you will notice several areas of recent cutting, in an attempt to encourage more wild life. Continue ahead for about 30-40 yards to where the track divides and take the right fork. Follow the very clear broad path, heading in a north-easterly direction. Pass a path going off to the right and then a path to the left, and reach a metal gate at the edge of the woods. Go through the gate and along the edge of the woods, with an open field to your right – and good view to the radio masts at Wychbold – and beyond. Stay close to the fence, passing a remnant of a sunken track and walk on to reach a metal kissing gate and the road.

3. Walk along the road for about 300 yards and at a main entrance to the woods, turn left, passing another information board. The broad track leads back into the heart of the woods, and after about a quarter mile rises slightly and passes a shed on the right of the path (and probably a pile of logs). Shortly beyond here at the cross paths, and a few yards before reaching a redwood tree, turn right. On the wooden signpost is the logo of the Royal Hunters Walk, one of the series of three Hunters Walks which extend from Bromsgrove. Walking through an area of silver birch, one of several varieties of trees seen in the wood, descend slightly to reach the edge of the woods and a smart metal gate.

4. Walk along the right edge of the field – with farm buildings to the right. Go through a gate and along the margin of the next field, to pass close to a large pylon. At a cross paths keep ahead and over the stiled footbridge. Head straight across the field towards a modern small metal gate and out on to the track. Through the large gate, the track leads up to the farm and the very smart converted barns. Enjoy the views looking back toward Chaddesley Woods. Pass through the large wooden gate and the old farmyard – now more of a courtyard parking area. Note the original farm house has been retained, on the left, with the old pump in front. Walk on along the farm drive, and as the track bends right, just before reaching the road, turn left. A modern bungalow is to your right, as you walk along the field margin. Move slightly right, and down a few steps, as the path leaves the field. Walk between gorse and a hedge to pass the small pools. Cross the middle of open fields heading towards the village with the church spire straight

ahead. Reach the stiled footbridge, and walk on, to the left of the Doctors' Surgery, through a small gate and slightly left along the road between modern houses. At the end of this road, turn right and return to the main street in the village.

View of the village

27. Feckenham

From the historic village of Feckenham, with its attractive houses and gardens, the walk takes you across countryside and round the Nature Reserve of Wylde Moor, a relic of a large former marshland.

Distance and time	4½ miles – 2 hours
Terrain	All gentle and fairly flat, on a track and clear paths. In the Wildlife Reserve the path may be soft and squelchy during wet spells of weather
How to get there	Along the B4090 between Droitwich and Alcester
Starting point	The well signed public free car park in the centre of the village, about 200 yards from the B4090. GR 009614
Refreshments	The Lygon Arms, a family owned Free House (phone 01527 893495)
Tourist Information Centres	Redditch (01527 60806) and Arrow Valley Countryside Centre (01527 464000)
Other places of interest	Hanbury Hall (01527 821214) and the Needle Museum in Redditch (01527 62509)
Maps	OS Landranger 150; Explorer 220

The ancient village of Feckenham is close to the border with Warwickshire, and much of its early growth was associated with making needles. Situated in the midst of a glorious rural area, the village was within the old Feckenham Forest where King John hunted. The Royal Hunting Lodge and the Forest Prison were situated just west of the present day village green. The village has largely escaped modern developments and contains buildings of different ages and different styles, including Georgian and half timbered. Several workshops and mills have survived, but are converted into modern-day houses.

Church of St John the Baptist

The sandstone church of St John the Baptist is noted for its short square tower and wide nave. Although partially rebuilt by Butterworth in 1853, a few Norman remnants have survived. Open daily, this well cared for church holds many features of interest, including an attractive collection of kneelers, and unusual 19th century geometric wall decoration, based on a medieval design. Medieval communion wafer tongs are still to be seen – securely padlocked, and notice the iron chest made from a single tree trunk.

Feckenham Wylde Moor covers 11 hectares and is one of Worcestershire Wildlife Trust's Nature Reserves. It is the remnant of an extensive marshland area in the valley of the Brandon Brook. The damp landscape is the result of the geological rock type of Keuper clay which retains water. The land was drained for farming in about 1850 but has been allowed to return to wetland, and has been a Nature Reserve since 1981, and now contains a small lake. Wild flowers and dragonflies are amongst the specialities of the area, with a range of birds inhabiting hedges and reedbeds. Snipe may be seen, and on the pool there may be ducks and little grebe, as well as reed buntings and the occasional sighting of a kingfisher. Animals sometimes graze parts of the reserve in the summer.

The Walk

1. From the car park walk back to the road and turn right, passing the Village Hall and many of the fine old houses which line the main street. At the T-junction opposite the Lygon Arms, ignore the footpath signed to Beanhall Mill and Morton Underhill, and turn left towards Alcester. After 150 yards along the narrow pavement, turn

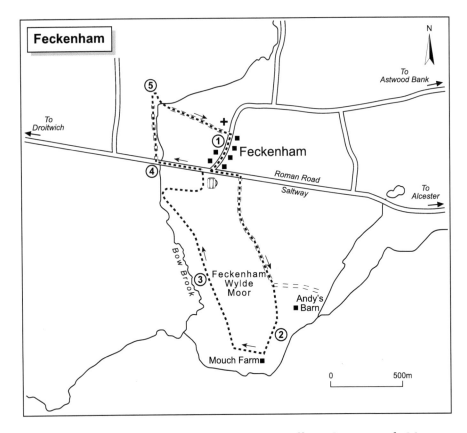

right along Moors Lane towards Bradley Green and Morton Underhill. The surfaced lane soon becomes a stony track and begins to descend. Pass the driveway to Beanhall Mill going right, and then the first entrance into the Nature reserve. Keep straight ahead towards Mouch Farm, and by a metal gate on the right is another entrance into the Reserve. Turn right here, and then immediately left, along the path through the trees, with the stony drive just a few yards to the left. Follow this path, with a wire fence on the right, and soon bend to the right as the path leads to the hide.

2. You are now on the signed Nature Trail which leads to the hide, looking out over the pool. Although only created in 1982, it is already a haven for wild life, with breeding reed buntings, little grebe, coot and moorhen. Mallard, Canada geese, occasionally a

swan, heron, and many visiting ducks can be seen on the pool, which is also home to great crested newts, toads and frogs. Sixteen species of dragonfly have been recorded. I was thrilled to see a kingfisher here on my most recent visit.

From the hide go on over the stile and follow the marker posts for the Nature Trail through lush vegetation. This is the edge of the marshy wetland area. Reeds, flowers, butterflies and many birds live here. Reed and sedge warblers are to be seen here in the summer. The path is likely to be soft as you follow the fringe of the wetland. The path bends right, when the buildings of Mouch Farm can be seen through the hedge to your left. Go on over a stile, with the very helpful tall handle pole, and continue along the fenced narrow path and, just before the next stile, turn left over a stiled footbridge. Then immediately turn right over two stiles and into a large field, which may contain rare breed sheep. Turn right here to stay close to the fence, with the Reserve through the hedge to your right. At the end of the large field, go on over a stile and across a small stream into the area of undergrowth and trees.

Pool by the bird hide

3. Reach a major cross paths and keep straight ahead in a northerly direction. After about 20 yards reach a driveway (which leads left to Beanhall) and keep straight ahead along a narrow bridleway into an area of young plantation of native broadleaved trees. These include silver birch, oak, spindle and many other varieties. A footpath crosses the bridleway but we keep straight ahead. Reach a modern metal gate, the first of several, with a high handle for horse riders to use. Keep straight ahead, with a wire fence on the left, and cross three small fields and pass to the left of a modern barn, into an area of small paddocks. Go diagonally left of straight ahead across the small fields to an older field boundary where we turn right, about 100 yards before reaching the houses of Feckenham. Go over a stile and along a clear path, with paddocks and then a barn and a horse exercise patch to our right, with houses clearly visible to the left. Turn left through a metal kissing gate, and into the car park of the Lygon Arms. Turn left along the main road, to pass the Village Shop on the left and a variety of old houses on the right, including the Old Black Boy, (formerly a pub on the Stage Coach route), Manor House and Saltway Cottage (the Old route to Droitwich).

4. Walk along the pavement and once beyond the bridge turn right, following the bridleway towards Ham Green and Cruise Hill. Pass a house on the left. The stream is to the right. We are soon much higher than the stream. Ignore paths crossing our route, and after about 500 yards reach a major cross paths.

5. Ahead is the path to Berrow Hill, the right turn is the Burial Way, but we turn sharp right signed to The Square. At a footbridge over the stream notice the ford a few yards to the right. The path bends left and climbs slightly to reach the first houses of Feckenham. This is Mill Lane and in the past there were two old mills alongside the stream we just crossed. On our left is the magnificent cricket pitch and shortly beyond here we reach The Square - with the church a few yards to the left. Attractive houses surround The Green and at the main road notice the white building opposite, with the arched windows. This was once a factory. Turn right along the road to return to the car park and the starting point.

28. Birlingham to Eckington

Across the flat land of the Avon valley, in the heart of the Vale of Evesham, this circular walk from Birlingham passes a Nature Reserve, crosses the Avon, and visits Eckington, whilst enjoying the ever present but changing views of Bredon Hill.

Distance and time	5 miles – gentle 2-3 hours, depending on frequency of stops to admire the view or look for birds and butterflies
Terrain	Mostly level though may be wet in places. No stiles have to be climbed
How to get there	Turn off the A4104 Upton on Severn to Pershore Road along the B4080 and then turn left on the minor road into Birlingham
Starting point	Near the church GR933432. Parking is available in the centre of the village
Refreshments	Birlingham village pub The Swan (01386 750485), or in the Bell Inn Eckington (01386 750033) pub, and a choice of eating places in Pershore
Tourist Information Centre	Pershore (01386 556591)
Other places of interest	Pershore with its historic abbey 3 miles to the north, and the village of Bredon 3 miles to the south
Maps	OS Explorer 190; Landranger 150

Birlingham is located around the church in the midst of rich farming countryside close to the River Avon. It includes a mix of modern and older houses – including a few with thatch. Before leaving the starting point, close to the church of St James and village hall, study the large map outside the village hall, which can provide much information about the village and surroundings. The church was largely rebuilt from 1871-72, but a Norman arch from the old church has been reused as the entrance to the churchyard. The tower is from the 15th century and the middle part has been used as a dovecote – for the Rector's pigeons. The interior consists of a large nave and two side chapels. The old stocks can be seen in the corner of the church. The churchyard is well known for its display of wild flowers, especially the carpet of snowdrops in February, followed by the purple crocuses and cyclamens. A noted vicar was Canon Duke and it was his daughter Eldie Duke who used to join the cutters to scythe the long grass each year, though not until after Whitsun, to prevent damaging the bulbs. Amongst the several fine trees in the churchyard is the fig to the side of the porch, planted by Canon Duke.

Gateway to the church

The walk

1. Walk along Church Street, passing a Picture Framer's house before reaching The Swan, the black and white thatched village pub. Parts of this delightful and welcoming pub date from the 1500s. The beamed interior and a warming fire is welcoming in winter and the south facing garden is a pleasure in the summer. This Free House serves home cooked food every day and can also offer darts or games of crib and dominoes. Follow the road and soon leave the

village, with the first of several wonderful views of Bredon Hill ahead. When the road bends left, we go right along the track across fields, to turn right just before the large barns. The paths throughout this walk are clearly signed. After 100 yards turn left, alongside the barn, to reach a gate by a stile (the stile can be avoided). Turn right along the narrow road and on the left is Hall Farm House. Just past the buildings turn left along the narrow footpath, and pass through a former cherry orchard as you head towards a long low building, with Bredon Hill beyond. Go on through a small metal gate, and pass to the right of the long low building, The Row, which dates from the 1820s. Continue to the

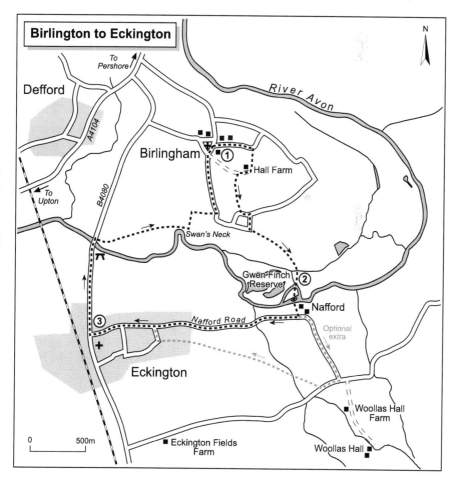

narrow road, and turn left and, after 50 yards turn right, along the narrow road, to pass the modernised building with a clock on the left. Follow this road, passing a few houses, to reach a T-junction and large sheds. Turn left here along Berwick Lane, which soon deteriorates into a track. Continue between fields, noticing over to the left the church in Great Comberton on the hill top. On the right are two windmills, as you reach the Gwen Finch Wetland Nature Reserve on our right. The information board tells you that this site was restored from 1999-2001, and now is the home for breeding redshanks, yellow wagtails and reed warblers, and otters have reappeared in this area. Coots, ducks, swans and geese also can be seen with many more duck such as wigeon coming here in the winter months. Cross over a stream, Berwick Brook, and walk along the field margin to reach the footbridge by the weir and shortly arrive at Nafford Lock.

2. Cross over the lock, and then over the River Avon by the weir and when the path ahead divides, take the narrow left fork. Climb

Nafford lock

steadily here, with the house and garden on the left. This is Nafford House which offers B and B. At the top of the climb is a narrow road. A few centuries ago there was a small village of Nafford but the village disappeared and the church was abandoned in the 16th century.

Possible extension walk: You could turn left here for an extension walk, along the road as far as the T-junction. At this junction a left turn would lead to the driveway up to Woollas Hall (which dates from 1661) and the location of the Deer Park Business Centre. But turn right and soon reach a footpath on the right, which crosses fields from Woollas Hall down to the Nafford Road.

But the main route from Nafford House is to turn right along the narrow country lane, and enjoy the good views looking down on the lakes in the Gwen Finch Reserve. The Malvern Hills and Bredon Hill are also clearly seen from the small Anglers'car park. Continue along Nafford Road for a mile (to be joined by the path from Woollas), to reach Eckington village, passing a variety of houses on the way. At the major road, B4080, opposite a war memorial and an old cross, turn right, but turn left here if visiting the village, the Bell Inn and the church of Holy Trinity with its 12th century Norman nave. One of the outstanding monuments inside is a memorial to John Hanford of Woollas Hall.

3. For the onward walk pass the war memorial on your left and keep ahead. Leave the village near the playing fields and make use of the footpath to the left of the road. Walk on down to the Eckington Wharf Picnic and Parking space, and the bridge over the river. There was formerly a ferry here, and then a bridge was built. The present bridge dates from 1720, and has cutwaters on both sides. Once beyond the bridge go right through the metal kissing gate, and head diagonally left across the middle of the large field. Look out for birds such as curlew or skylark in this ham, the floodplain meadow. At the far side go on through another metal gate signed 'Eckington Wharf Circular Walk and Shakespeare's Avon Way'. The latter is an 88 mile walk from the source near Naseby to the confluence with the Severn in Tewkesbury. Turn right along the track, passing old willow trees on the right. Also on the right is the river, with the sharp meander known as Swan's Neck. After

about 150 yards, and at the end of the field reach a T-junction and turn left, following a clearly signed path. At the next T-junction turn right and the track becomes surfaced as you pass the very smart modernised buildings (Bell Barn, Waggoners Cottage) on the right to reach a road near the Manor House. Turn left along Lower End and this road leads back to the church and the centre of the village.

View to the Malverns

29. Great Malvern and Worcestershire Beacon

Beginning from the centre of Great Malvern and passing blue plaques, which provide memories of Malvern's Victorian Water Cure, walk up to the highest point of the hills. On the way to the Worcestershire Beacon (height 425m) climb via St Ann's Well and Rushy Valley, and descend past the Gold Mine stone and Earnslaw Quarry.

Distance and time	6 miles (less if starting from the town car parks). Time required up to 3 hours
Terrain	The walk is on pavements and good clear paths, mainly climbing in the first half and descending in the second half
How to get there	From junction 7 on the M5 and follow signs to Malvern
Starting point	Great Malvern station (GR 784456) or perhaps in the town centre near The Splash Sports Centre and adjacent to the car park
Refreshments	A good choice in Great Malvern
Tourist Information Centre	Malvern (01684 892289)
Other places of interest	The Herefordshire town of Ledbury and the Severnside town of Upton
Maps	Harvey's map of Malvern (1:10,000 scale) available from the Malvern TIC or Upton upon Severn map shop; OS Explorer 190

The walk

1. No town walk in Malvern would be complete without a visit to Great Malvern station, with the handsome Victorian features as well as 'the worm', the tunnel used by Victorian visitors to reach the Imperial Hotel without having to go out on the street. From the station walk to Avenue Road, nearly opposite the imposing Imperial, now part of the Girls school Malvern St James. Turn left and walk into the town passing the selection of trees – more than ten varieties in the grassy square outside the station with many more along the road and in the large gardens. At the corner of Priory Road is a monkey puzzle tree where a left turn will lead to the entrance to The Splash. Turn in here and walk through the park and beyond the steps to the theatre entrance, and round the left side of the buildings. This leads past the Handkerchief tree, one of many specimen trees in the Park.

Anne Darwin gravestone in Priory churchyard

Cross the road and walk through the Priory churchyard, with yet more trees of interest including Mediterranean evergreen oak, Monterey pine, and Lebanon cedar. Anne Darwin's grave is in this churchyard. Climb slightly up to Belle Vue, passing the Elgar Statue and the Malvhina spring, cross the main road and turn right for a few yards. At the ancient pub, The Unicorn, a former coaching Inn, notice the Civic Society plaque recalling links with CS Lewis. Turn round to walk back along the pavement, passing Robson Ward, and in their courtyard is the Chalybeate well, the site of the first water to be bottled in Malvern. At Lloyds Bank notice another Civic

Society plaque telling us that Dr Wilson was here, during the time of the Victorian Water Cure. Next door is the Mount Pleasant Hotel, with the recently restored bowl from St Ann's Well outside the side entrance from the car park. Note the old Orangery at the top of the garden. Turn right into Rose Bank Garden, the site of the old Rose Bank House, which was demolished in 1959. Climb the 99 steps (only 95 really) and at the half way point, at step 47 there are already good views opening up over the town. At the top of the steps turn left, and then right, to follow the steep and winding road up to St Ann's Well. The cottage at the well was built in 1815 and the octagonal mushroom shaped buildings added in 1843. The

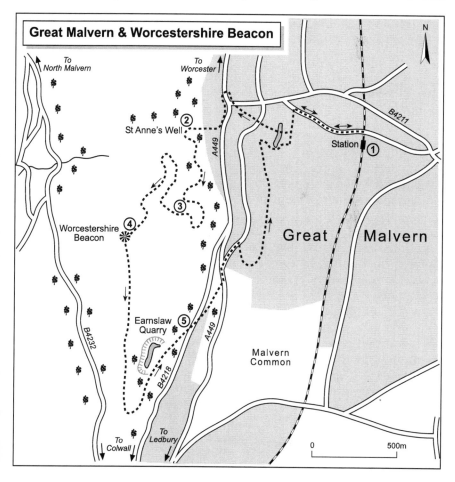

popular café provides drinks and snacks and the information boards give a little of the history.

2. Turn left at St Ann's Well along the broad and level path above the grass roofed toilet block. Just past a zig-zag path going down to the left, the main path bends right. After a few more yards fork right off this main path and begin to climb on the narrow path. This crosses the steep Rushy Valley, with its short stretch of a rock river. Clearance work and tree felling have taken place in Rushy Valley, as part of the ongoing necessary management to keep views open as well as creating different habitats for wild life. Good views open up across Malvern, notably to the old Imperial Hotel and Christ Church spire. The path climbs gradually up the slope, through an area with bilberry plants. Views open up across the plain, with fields of bright yellow rape being dominant in spring, and then the buildings of Qinetiq and the playing fields of Malvern College can be seen. These are two important features of Malvern's history as the town is famous for its schools, and in World War II was very famous for its work on the development of radar. Qinetiq is the modern name for the important company working on scientific research.

3. Reach a T-junction by an old green iron seat – turn right here and continue climbing slightly, to emerge above the trees. The path bends left, round a rocky outcrop to the left of the path, with the steep Rushy Valley down to the right. The path leads round the top of Rushy Valley – with lots of bilberries here. Pass the Dripping Well on the left, and as usual it is dripping. The water supply attracts a variety of birds – including robins, willow warblers, stonechat, linnet, wren. The path undulates slightly as it curves round the top of the valley, passing over several rocky outcrops. Reach a major path and turn left here to continue climbing. Follow this broad grassy path, with St Ann's Well down to the right and North Hill across to the right. Bend sharp left when this path divides and climb steadily, passing above the top of Rushy Valley. By a seat on the left, the path takes a sharp right bend to lead on up to the top of the Worcestershire Beacon. Different birds may be seen in this open grassy area, with pipits, and perhaps stonechats, on the gorse. Follow the main path up to the Beacon and the toposcope, from where wonderful views look across the

countryside in all directions. Then take the surfaced track and follow this downhill towards the Wyche Cutting.

4. On the way from the Beacon, notice the large West Malvern quarries down to the right, and then reach the area of trees again. Colourful gorse may be in flower on the left of the path and grass with bluebells on the right of the path. The views ahead look to Pinnacle Hill, the Herefordshire Beacon, Eastnor Obelisk, with the Herefordshire and Welsh hills away to the right.

Toposcope on the summit of the Beacon – east side

At the round marker stone at the site of the so-called Gold mine, turn left here following the sign to Quarry walks and Earnslaw. When this path divides take the right fork alongside a small wall round the top of a former quarry. Descend quite steeply through the woods. Reach an open area and the major path where you continue downhill on a stony track – but first perhaps go up the steps on the left to look down into Earnslaw Quarry lake, or go on a few yards and round to the left to reach the lake and the useful information board. Continue on downhill and soon reach the memorial seat to Con and Lena very close to the main Wyche road.

5. Go down to the road here, cross over and move 20 yards to the left to reach a path which goes down to a narrow road. Keep straight ahead across this road and follow the path through the woods down to the Wells Road. Turn left here and fork right along Abbey Road, passing what used to be the Ellerslie section of Malvern College on the left – now awaiting redevelopment. Notice the Civic Society plaque on the wall just inside the gate. Take the first right, College Road, and follow this road as it bends to the left and passes the main sections of Malvern College on the right. Just past School House is House No. 9 with a blue plaque

commemorating Dr CP Rowe CBE. At the end of College Road go straight ahead across to Orchard Road with its fluted pillar box dating from 1857, and one of three in Malvern. Walk on towards the park and theatre. Just before reaching the entrance to the park, turn right along the footpath and this will lead through to Priory Road, the Splash Car park and then on to the station, if required. Before reaching Priory Road the house on the right is Spa Cottage, the site of a chalybeate spring, and on its wall is another Civic Society plaque. Turn left here to return to the car park or to the station.

30. Elmley Castle

Walk from this delightful village, set in glorious countryside, and pass close to the site of the castle to climb the hilltop. Follow the ridge top as you walk on to the tower and old iron age hill fort, whilst enjoying the stunning all-round views.

Distance and time	6 miles; time required 3 hours
Terrain	Mostly dry and firm paths through woods and over grassland. Long but steady climb from Elmley Castle, rewarded by wonderful views – and ends with the descent back into the village
How to get there	From Pershore along the B4084 towards Evesham. Cross the River Avon near the old Pershore bridge and as the main road bends left, turn right towards Little Comberton and then Elmley Castle
Starting point	GR 983410 the church, or GR 984412 the picnic place
Refreshments	Queen Elizabeth pub in Elmley Castle (01386 710839) and pubs in Bredon; good choice of pubs and tea shops in Pershore, Evesham or Tewkesbury
Tourist Information Centres	Pershore (01386 556591); Evesham (01386 446944)
Other places of interest	Pershore Abbey; Evesham Almonry
Maps	OS Explorer 190; Landranger 150

Elmley Castle
The old castle was just outside the present village and was built by the Despenser family in the 11th century – later used by the Beauchamps.

Largely abandoned by 14th century but later restored and finally abandoned in the 16th century. Little remains, but an embankment can be seen from the path as you climb the hill.

The church is at one end of the village and close by are several black and white cottages, and also the old Village Hall with its stone ground floor but timber framed upper parts. The village cross is at the other end of the village. Some modern development has taken place. The Queen Elizabeth (phone 01386 710839), opposite the Village Hall, has been recently renovated, and the old sign remains – for August 20th, to commemorate the visit of the Queen in 1575, when she stayed with the Savage family – the Lords of the Manor at that time.

The church of St Mary dates back to the 11th century (note the herring bone stone work in the chancel) – but otherwise dates from 13th and 15th centuries. Amongst the interesting features inside the church is a remarkable alabaster monument to the Savage family, from about 1700. The font is 15th century on a 13th base, with dragons. The rabbit and pig in the porch are of Norman age. Outside can be seen the fortified tower, and two decorated sundials in the churchyard, one of which is showing the Savage coat of arms.

Carving of rabbit on the right hand side of the church entrance porch

The Walk

1. Start from the path to the left of the church, passing a pond on your right and go on over a stile. Walk along the fenced path to another stile and then turn right. Follow the right margin of this large field, as it bends to the left. Parkland is to the right, extending up the slope leading to Castle Hill. At the end of the field go right over a footbridge and stile, and head towards the far left corner of the field – probably with sheep and perhaps horses for company. Leave the field over a stile and small footbridge then

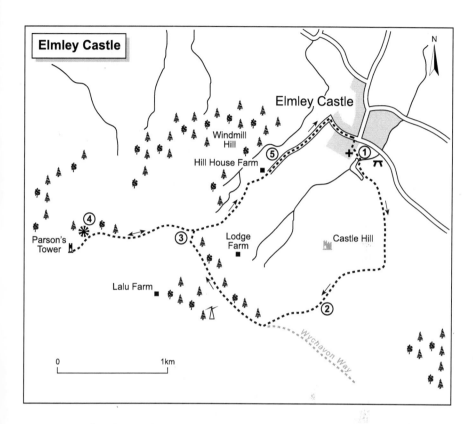

turn right through the metal gate to follow the bridleway uphill –
now on Wychavon Way, with a 'W' logo. Pass a small elongated lake
on the left. Wild life is abundant on Bredon Hill, including many
varieties of butterflies, some dragonflies and many birds,
including spotted flycatchers. Continue to climb, with Castle Hill
to the right. Fork right when the path splits, still following the W',
and pass through a few trees, including some very tall ash. Grass
and patches of bracken are the ground cover. Continue the ascent
bending slightly right over another footbridge, and then bending
to the left. You may see a small gate over to your right – with a
notice saying 'No Walkers'. Ignore a path going left, and keep
ahead through a few trees, with open grassland to the left and a
wire fence to the right. Enjoy good views to Castle Hill on the right
and long views back across the plain to the Cotswold scarp (with
Meon Hill at the left end)

2. Reach a modern metal gate and enter the woods. The climb continues through the mixed deciduous woods on a path littered with fragments of Cotswold stone. Reach a dog leg in the path by a large gate and private land, but just keep on climbing to reach the large wooden gate at the top edge of the woods. Here is a major cross paths – and stunning views especially to the south – Dumbleton Hill and the Cotswold scarp with the masts on Cleeve Hill. May Hill with its distinctive clump of trees will also be seen on a clear day. The Wychavon Way bends sharp left to descend to Ashton under Hill, straight ahead leads towards Overbury, but turn right on the footpath between the edge of the woods and a wire fence. Follow this for half a mile, passing the coniferous wood and large telecommunications mast to the left, then a cross paths with a right turn into the woods and the path left leading to Lalu Farm. Continue ahead to the edge of the woods and a gate.

3. Here, keep straight ahead for just over half a mile to visit the tower on the top of the hill. The wire fence is on your left and lone hawthorn trees to the right. Keep ahead to a small clump of coniferous trees and a gate, and the tower will be in sight. Pass through the gate and walk on. Look out for the Malvern Hills ahead and the dishes of the radar station at Defford down to the right. The two villages of Comberton as well as Pershore will be clearly visible down to the right.

4. Continue straight ahead towards the tower at point number 4. Often known as Parson's Folly, the tower dates from the late 18th century when it was built by Mr Parson of Kemerton Court, in order that the hilltop should reach the height of 1000 feet. As you approach the tower, pass a large ditch and embankment which surround the old fort to the left. Over the wall on

18th century hilltop tower

Rock in the shape of the elephant

our right is a very steep drop. From the tower, at a height of 299m (981 ft), Cleeve Hill and its masts are 9 miles away, and the Worcestershire Beacon on the Malverns is 12 miles distant. Close to the tower the Banbury Stone sits in a deep hollow, and has been called the elephant stone because of its shape when viewed from one side. Local legends suggest it might have been a sacrificial stone for druids, but it is merely a natural outcrop.

Bredon Hill is a residual hill, an outlier of the Cotswolds and a relic of the time when the Cotswold scarp extended several miles further west. Isolated hills such as Bredon have been left behind because they are slightly harder than the surrounding rocks which have been eroded during the last few million years.

Retrace steps to point 3.

176 Walks in Three Choirs Counties

For the onward route follow the edge of the woods downhill. Turn right at a track, and after a few yards reach a cross tracks. The path from the woods on your right heads down a sunken path towards the Combertons and Bricklehampton, but keep straight ahead and descend steadily. This slope was the site of an old quarry and is a wonderful nature reserve, especially rich in wild flowers which love this alkaline soil. Pass a gate on the right which leads to Lodge Farm, but keep straight ahead – enjoying views all around. The lower ground ahead is likely to be showing fields of golden cereals. Pass through a wooden gate and continue descending quite steeply.

5. Then drop down to a cross paths, and bend slightly to the right, not the first on the right but the second and narrower path which continues the descent, towards the woods. Reach a wooden gate and enter the woods and follow the sunken track – which may have originally been used as access to the quarry you have just walked through. This section could be muddy in wet weather. Reach the end of the surfaced road, with the driveway to Lodge Farm on the right and Hill House Farm to the left. Two or three parking places here are often used by walkers. Pass a few thatched cottages and black and white houses along the roadside (Hill Lane) as it bends right to enter the village. The old Village Hall is straight ahead as you return to the church.